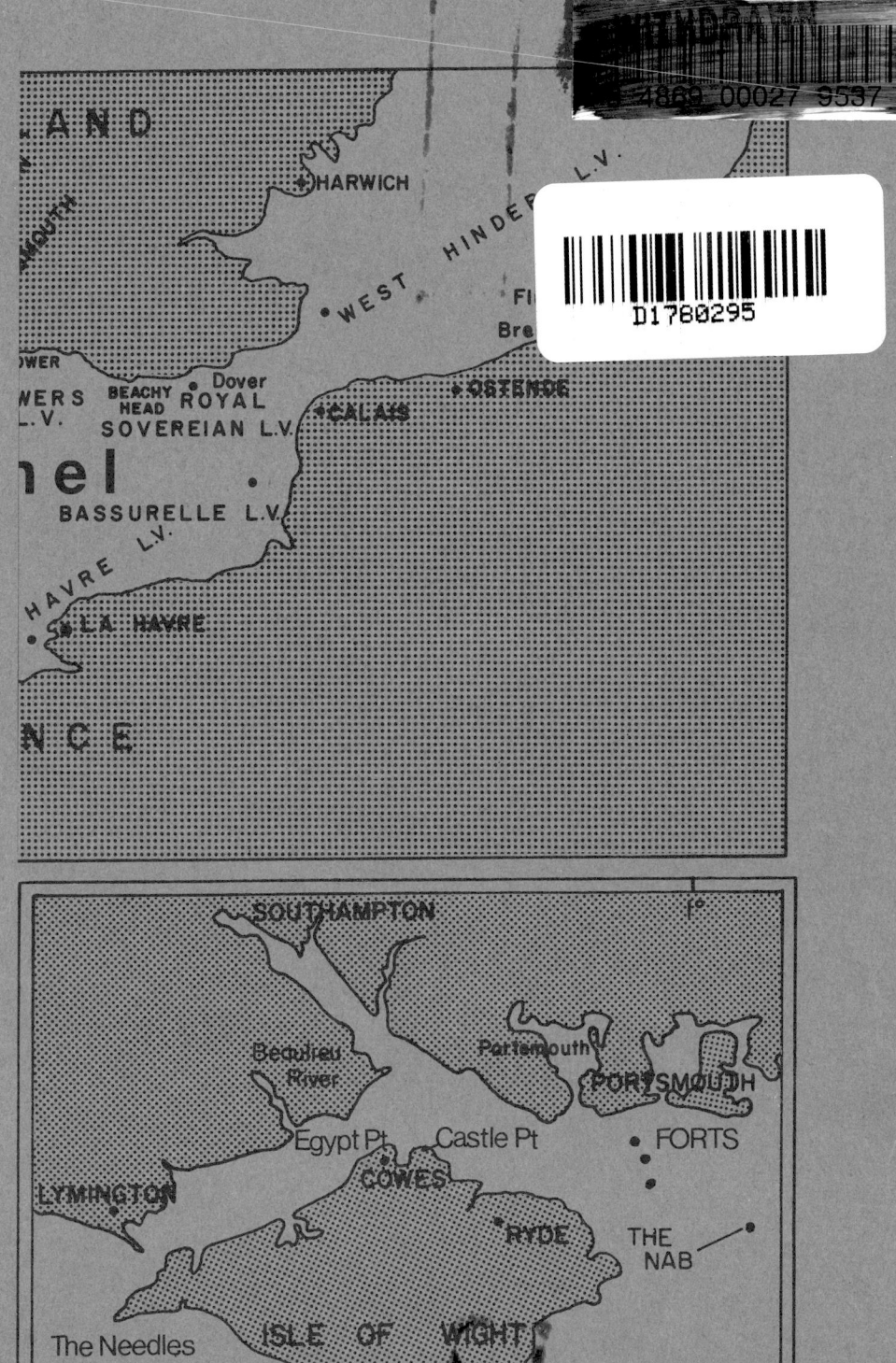

The Leading Edge

Barre Publishers · Barre, Massachusetts

The Leading Edge

Sandy Weld

Introduction by John Carter

Title page: Red Rooster *approaching Fastnet Rock*

© 1971 by Barre Publishing Co., Inc.
All rights reserved
Library of Congress Catalog Number 71-154060
Standard Book Number 8271-7102-1
Printed in the United States of America

Table of Contents

Introduction	vii
1. Tuning *Rabbit*	3
2. To Cowes	25
3. Dinard to Le Havre	38
4. First One Ton Cup	47
5. Cowes Week	57
6. Fastnet	67
7. Gearing Down	77
8. Australia	85
9. Thar She Blows	101
10. *Tina*	109
11. *Rabbit II*	133
12. *Red Rooster*	149
Appendix: The New Rule	181

Credits

Illustrations not otherwise credited were made by the author. Jim Anderson: 68, 152 (top). *Bâteaux:* 21, 31, 46, 70, 137, 148, 162 (bottom), 173. Beken of Cowes: 56, 135 (top), 140, 156. *The Cork Examiner:* title pages. Pierre Fouquin: 108. Alain Gliksman: 145. Taylor Grant: 179. *The Mercury:* 84, 90, 96, 99. *Modern Boating:* 162 (top). Eileen Ramsey: 135 (bottom), 139. *Yachting World:* 132, 136, 166. *Yachts and Yachting:* 7. Charts by courtesy of Cruising Club of Australia (91, 93) and Royal Ocean Racing Club and *Yachting World* (15, 32, 38, 58, 66, 71, 170).

Introduction

OCEAN racing boats have probably changed more in the last ten years than anytime since racing yachts took to the ocean courses. Some of the change is related to materials: dacron sails and cordage; steel, aluminum, and fiberglass hulls; and the advance in electronic equipment. A large part of the change has been an assault on what, within a given rating rule, makes a boat go faster. This change has been so sweeping, the assault so effective, that it has led to a new international rating rule (I.O.R.).

Here is a personal view of those events and an account of one of the most incredibly successful individual records ever made by a designer and skipper. In 1965 Dick Carter was a skillful skipper, but an unknown amateur designer. Today he is one of the leading designers in the world and one of the formulators of the new international rating rule.

Sandy Weld has played a key role in this transformation as he helped prepare and sail *Rabbit* in 1965 for a summer's campaign, then joined *Tina* in Copenhagen for the 1966 One Ton Cup competition and two Admiral's Cup challenges on board *Rabbit II* and *Red Rooster*. In between he was fortunate enough to tuck in two other great races literally a world apart—the Bermuda race and the Sydney-Hobart race in Australia.

His account of the rapid design changes, the exciting boats on some of the great racing courses of the world is delivered in a modest, understated New England way.

Each year competition gets more difficult, demanding more concentration, greater attention to detail, and greater skill in steering and sail trimming. Fewer mistakes are tolerable if one is to win. As the intensity of racing increases, the ancient battle with fatigue and the need to think clearly and logically continue and become more critical—placing more and more importance on the crew.

Top boats must have skilled crews. The ability to concentrate and to fight fatigue must be in each member. Sometimes the spirit or the drive that lets a crew extend itself is a group product, but more often it comes from an individual within the crew. You know him: the first on deck at a watch change, the first to react to trouble, the first to remember after a period of prolonged stress that we all need food and then produce it. . . . the man who overcomes the inertia of the "way things are." This sort of man, a person of many skills, is the "motor" that makes a good boat and crew tops. Sandy is a great "motor" and a great ship mate. This is his account of top flight ocean racing—the sport's "leading edge."

John A. Carter

The Leading Edge

Rabbit's *launching at Breskens*

1. Tuning *Rabbit*

I arrived at the Maas Boat Yard in Breskens, Holland, during the middle of a drizzly Friday afternoon at the end of May 1965. It was my first meeting with Dick Carter and *Rabbit*. *Rabbit* wasn't hard to find, sitting in her cradle on the edge of the quay with a half dozen men working on and around her at a feverish pace. Dick I found in a nearby shed checking over the spar. Our greetings were short; time was of the essence, for many things had still to be accomplished, supervised, and checked. I spent the rest of the afternoon following him about in awe. He dealt with one detail after another, from the placement of equipment to the color of paint for the interior.

Pressure was on to meet the launching schedule the next morning. Major projects included stepping the mast, rigging it, and reinstalling the depth sounder under the stern rather than where the equipment manufacturers indicated, the smooth leading edge of the forefoot.

Tasks, of which there were many, were completed so that when the riggers went home (long after the yard had closed for the day) we were basically ready for launching in the morning. Dick and I stayed busy on *Rabbit* long after the riggers had departed. We sorted out equipment, and in the process made lists of things still to be done, lists of things to be changed, lists of questions, and lists for the lists.

After dark Dick and I found our way to a small restaurant. It overlooked the harbor, which was filled with fishing vessels and sailing craft. Over dinner I learned about *Rabbit* and the hopes for the coming summer.

The plan was to have our first sail on Sunday, in two days' time, and then spend a couple more days in the yard before departing Tuesday noon for Harwich, England, and the North Sea Race. This was to be a shakedown race, after which we would return to the yard for the finishing details before shifting our headquarters to Cowes, England. From Cowes we would participate in the Morgan Cup, Cowes-Dinard Race, Channel Race, and Cowes Week, ending the season with the Fastnet Race. This was all very tentative: some races might be dropped; others, like the One Ton Cup, might be added. It all depended on *Rabbit*'s performance. The summer's goal was the Class III championship (awarded to the boat in Class III with the highest number of points in her best four Royal Ocean Racing Club races).

This summer's campaign had been touched off two years before when Dick was loaned a 32-foot Medalist for the 1963 Fastnet Race. That race started in one of those wild sou'westers, providing a rough beat out through the Needles. Conditions were made even tougher by the strong outgoing tide. Even though the boat was one of the smallest in the fleet they held down the middle of the Channel to get the maximum effect of the strong favorable tide, while most of the fleet sought smoother waters close to shore. It was a tough first night, but the last night was even wilder and more exhilarating. A front caught them as they passed the Lizard on their way in. With a storm spinnaker up, the only boat carrying a spinnaker, they surged in to Plymouth on one wave after another, often with two people on the helm.

The Medalist was noted for her hard downwind steering, a point of sailing which particularly intrigued Dick. His past efforts in racing dinghies and offshore had always been concentrated on the sails and trim to get the most out of a given hull. The importance of improving downwind sailing turned his thoughts to changes in the hull. This was the first step in the transformation from the sailor Carter to the designer Carter.

He spent the next year or so analyzing hulls, trying to determine for himself what made a boat go fast. Other aspects also came under close scrutiny, such as wind conditions, race courses, and of course the rating rule. The whole concept of transferring one's three-dimensional ideas onto two-dimensional paper with pen and ink so a builder could transform them into reality was nearly too much for him. With determination he put himself into a position where he had to produce a design: he made a "payment of intent" to Frans Maas Nv. in Holland to build a boat.

Then came a cable from Holland: NEED LINE PLANS IMMEDIATELY. Not a line had yet been placed on paper! His one drawing course at

Yale had only taught him to draw straight lines; how was he to draw a boat with its many complicated curves? Somehow, though, he did it.

As he tells it, the excitement was almost unbearable as the ferry crossed the river Schelde to Breskens. How would *Rabbit* look in the flesh, as a three-dimensional shape, something one could walk around, climb on, and even go inside? When Frans Maas drove him to the yard, and there *Rabbit* was sitting on the quay, all he could say was "She looks like a boat! She looks like a boat!" Frans shrugged his shoulders as if to say "Why not?"

In studying ocean racing courses Dick concluded that the vast majority of one's sailing time is spent with sheets eased rather than beating to windward. He also observed that when beating in an offshore race one was more than likely to experience a wind change prior to reaching the windward mark. His conclusion was that pure out-and-out boat speed when close reaching to running was more important than a boat's ability to claw to windward. The English had acquired the reputation for close-winded sailing as a result of racing around the tide-infested Solent where a degree or two could mean the advantage of a lee bow tide or not.

When studying the courses he also looked at weather conditions throughout the Channel and Fastnet Rock areas. The analysis showed clearly that these areas have their fair share of light and variable wind. The ominous reports of the English Channel gales are true enough, but no one talks of the calms between them. Dick made a point of "over-canvassing" *Rabbit* in relation to boats of a similar size. This was to give her added power in light conditions where valuable time can be gained while distances are covered slowly. On the other hand, he has the greatest respect for the sea and was determined that *Rabbit* be competent in the worst weather the Fastnet could dish out. After all, one does not win races when hove to.

Part of the problem in carrying on during a gale is the stamina of the crew, and stamina depends on the physical and mental condition of the crew members as they step on board. During long offshore races this condition is affected by many things; one major factor is rest. Rest can best be obtained, or not lost, when the boat is sailed in a relatively upright position rather than on its ear, with the lee rail awash: one expends less energy moving around on deck as well as below. One also rests better in his bunk when the boat isn't straining and at all angles.

Rabbit was designed to be sailed upright. This was not for her crew's sake, but because a boat's optimum speed is obtained when it is sailed in an upright position. Driving the boat hard with more sail than anyone else is dramatic, but it does very little for the speed of the boat.

The concepts that went into *Rabbit* were a low rating, and a proportionally fast boat in light to moderate winds and off the wind, capable of withstanding Fastnet's toughest weather. The result was a $34' \times 24' \times 10' \times 4'$ steel sloop. Her underwater body was a departure from the popular meter boat concept of reducing wetted surface to the minimum. She had very round bilges. The thickness of the keel where it joined the hull was a mere 6 inches.

Rabbit's 4-foot draft was so shallow in relation to the size of her hull that when the rating was calculated she received a "shallow-draft" bonus. The draft was the minimum allowed under the rating rule without incurring a penalty. *Rabbit*'s stability was achieved through hull design rather than placing large quantities of lead as low as possible. The keel itself was fairly short and on its trailing edge was attached a small rudder, or trim tab. This innovation was new to me, but not to sailing. Designers have been experimenting with it since the late forties. Well aft of the keel and attached only to the hull hung a balanced spade rudder. This was the means of directional control. The trim tab was used for additional directional control when on a reach or to provide lift when going to windward—very much like the lift created by flaps on an airplane wing. Electronic equipment consisted of the depth sounder (which hardly ever worked) and the radio/direction finder. No fancy electronic wind indicators were used; just simple foolproof yarn tied to the stays. Simplicity was a theme throughout *Rabbit*.

Rabbit's *original bow pulpit. Note how securely one can wedge oneself into the pulpit with feet and legs, leaving both hands free.*

The spar was designed by Carter and built at Hood's Yard. Ted Hood commented at the time, "Even the 12-meters don't do it this way." A simple principle was used in designing it: remove all windage possible, keeping in mind that it had to stand up in the Fastnet's toughest. The result was that all tangs, fittings that attach the shrouds to the mast, were internal. All halyards were internal, including the spinnaker halyard. The normal lower forward shrouds were eliminated and replaced by placing one stay as a lower forestay. With a luff groove the spar presented practically no unnecessary windage. Any theoretical advantage, however small, was tackled as being extremely important, so that the aggregate could amount to something measurable. This was the first offshore spar to have everything internal.

Probably the biggest single innovation on the spar was the indented roller reefing gear. Roller reefing has most definitely taken over from the reef points and the task of tying in a reef, but it still isn't the easy task it should be. This is primarily due to the so-called "roller reefing set back," which still requires many hands to accomplish the job efficiently and quickly. By indenting the reefing mechanism into the mast it was hoped that with the tack attached nearly underneath the luff groove reefing and unreefing would become a simple one-man job. The elimination of slides and jacklines would make reefing and unreefing easier.

Another novel feature on *Rabbit* was her bow pulpit. It was a solid, four-legged structure secured to the deck aft of the headstay. Its purpose was to give a solid structure from which to work when on the foredeck. The conventional pulpits, on small boats in particular, are anything but solidly built or very well secured to the boat. The rule concerning lifelines stated that they must consist of metal tubing or wire, or a combination of both, encompassing bow and stern without a break at a height of 2 feet from the deck. This is under the title "Seaworthiness and Regulations," and the obvious reason for having lifelines and pulpits is safety: a fence to keep the crew on board. Did it matter that the "fence" encompass every part of the hull? Apparently not, for recent practice had moved lifelines inside of side stays and stern pulpits inside of backstays on many of the new racing boats without any infringement of the rule. In defining the "bow," Webster's Dictionary refers to it as an area, "the forward part of a ship," rather than a specific point. Dick was satisfied that he had improved the device and complied with the rule as it was written. More important, he had increased the safety at sea which was the reason for the rule.

Beside being safer, it allowed the headsails to be set outside of the pulpit. This would alleviate the plaguing problem of the sail leading up over a conventional pulpit and lifelines. The practical benefit of this was that it reduced one of ocean sailing's major problems—chafe along the foot of the sail. The psychological advantage, however, outweighed the practical advantage in that *Rabbit* would have an unbroken marriage between sail and hull.

A year and a half of analyzing all this, countless changes, worries, and sleepless nights, resulted, finally, in our being in Holland. The Frans Maas Nv. Yard was selected to build in partly because the Dutch had more experience in welding thin gauge steel than anyone else, and partly because Frans, being a young designer, ocean racer, and builder, talked Dick's language. Dick was impressed with the construction of *Tonnere de Breskens,* a Maas design of the previous year. When a question arose that Dick wasn't sure of, his answer was "Do it as in *Tonnere.*" But no amount of assurance from Frans, who is a little more used to such launchings than Dick, could relieve his nervous anxiety. Would *Rabbit* actually float? Would she be anywhere near her designed waterline? Would she sail like a sailboat? If she actually behaved like a boat would she be competitive, or would he have to take the next plane home? After all, who ever heard of a man with no training at all designing his first boat and expecting it to sail well?

Night was well along before we turned in. I could have listened to Dick much longer, but we had to launch by noon the next day and be ready for our first sail Sunday. The moment of truth had arrived, with a busy time ahead of us.

Activity on *Rabbit* had begun when I arrived on the scene at eight o'clock Saturday morning. There seemed to be a never-ending amount of work to be performed and a rapidly decreasing time in which to do it all.

Shortly before noon *Rabbit* floated free from the railway. It didn't take long to get to the other dock to check out her flotation. She not only stayed afloat, she was floating very near her designed waterline level. Dick was thrilled, but wasn't allowed to gloat long, for there was too much yet to be done and there were too many decisions still to be made.

That afternoon the compass adjuster came around to adjust our two bulkhead compasses. The drill was to power out into the river mouth and swing around to known fixes on land. This we performed, but not in the orthodox manner. We had to power backward. The special folding propeller, shipped specially from California, U.S.A., had a right-handed pitch. The Norwegian engine required a left-handed pitch propeller to propel us forward. To run the engine in reverse to run the boat forward would have placed undue strain on the engine. So—the engine was in forward, but the boat went backward. Even though the compass adjuster seemed amused and confused by the goings-on, the compasses were adjusted and we survived our first

Rabbit

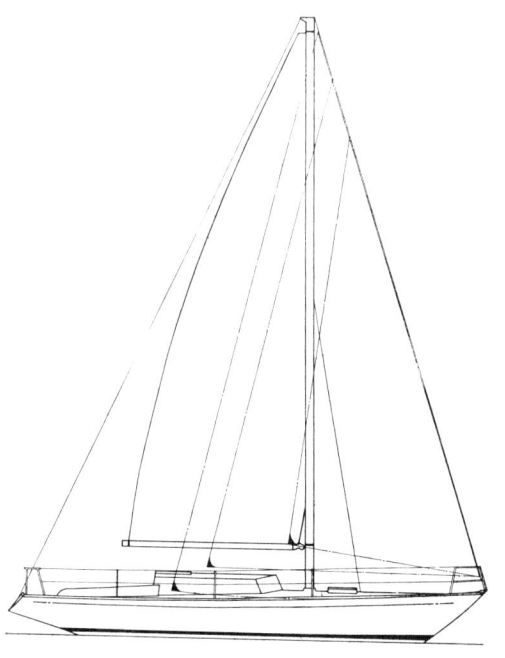

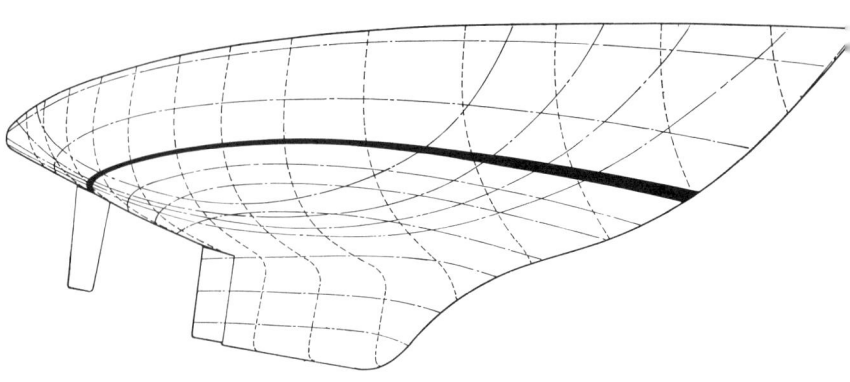

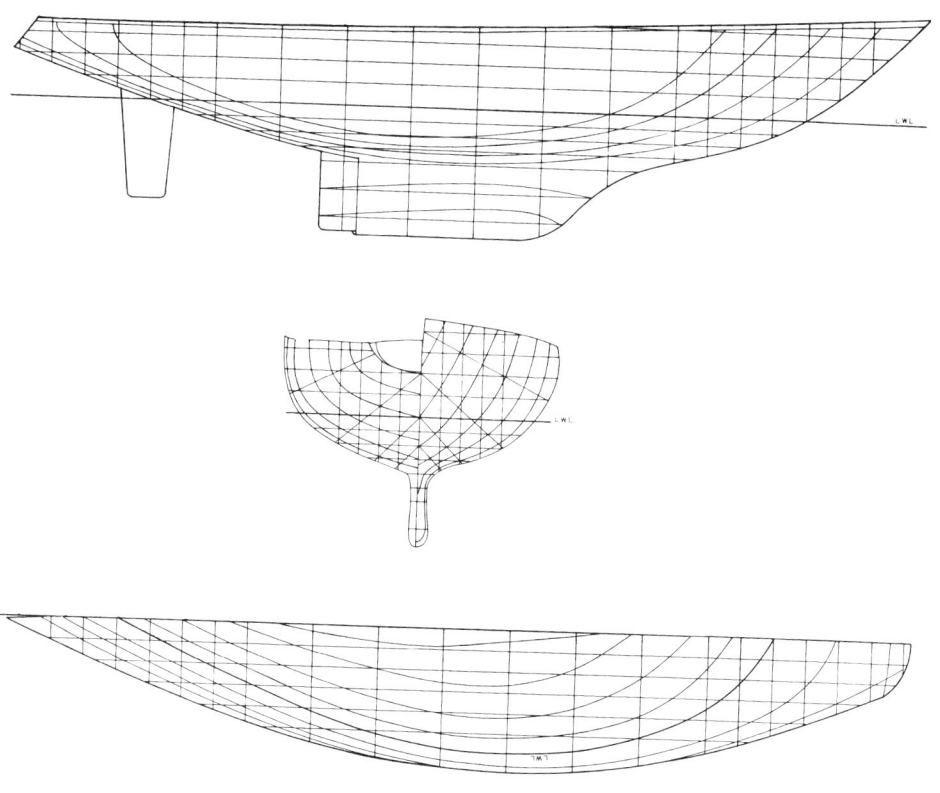

outing. An additional entry was made on one of the many lists: cable for a correctly pitched propeller.

Sunday morning arrived overcast and cold, normal for Holland at this time of year. Neither Dick nor I noticed the weather; we were too tied up in *Rabbit*'s first sail. Powering out of the harbor, again backward, we presented an odd sight to the few folks along the harbor entrance who were fishing, were on their way to church, or had just come down to the water.

The main was put on the boom; the outhaul gear wasn't big enough, for I broke the wire running up inside the boom when I tried to get the sail hauled out. That was one experiment that didn't quite work. A jury rig was devised to hold the sail in place and the main was raised. The luff groove arrangement worked all right, but it would have been easier with a couple more hands and more practice. I was too busy straightening things out to see a smile spread across Dick's face as *Rabbit* fell off and began to gather speed. She wasn't about to turn turtle, and she responded to wind and tiller. Up with the #2 genoa and we seemed to take off.

We sailed back and forth off Breskens. Two major questions had been successfully answered: she floated on her waterline, and she sailed with normal responses. The big question remained: would she be competitive?

Monday and Tuesday, work continued at a feverish pace. An amazing amount had been accomplished, but *Rabbit* was far from a finished product. The yard was happy that she was to return after the North Sea Race so that they could complete the work. It wasn't until 1700 hours that we finally pushed off, having found a left-handed pitch fixed-blade propeller to propel us in the right direction until we could get another one from California.

On board for the passage with us was a Dutch lad just out of the Dutch marines. Mike had little racing experience, but brought a long heritage of water life, and an abundance of youthful energy. We were glad to have him: beside being another pair of hands, he had a light and heart-warming personality. We motored all night through a lumpy calm sea. By 0800 Wednesday morning we had the Galloper Light Ship abeam. After breakfast the wind came in from the northeast, and we sailed along at a comfortable 6 knots. With the sun out, it was almost warm by noon. What a joyful sail into Harwich harbor! During the trip new lists started: one for things to do and get in Harwich before the race, and another list of things to be done upon our return to Breskens. On entering Harwich we tied up alongside some other racers beside the Trinity House flagship.

Thursday and Friday morning we were busy hurrying around buying necessary equipment and provisions for our first race. We still didn't know how she went in relation to other boats; we hadn't seen a sailboat when under sail ourselves.

We visited a marine store in town in order to gather the navigational equipment—charts, tide information, parallel rule, and dividers—and some snap shackles. They didn't have what we wanted in stock, but would send to London to get it.

The Trinity House ship didn't like us tied up to her and requested that we anchor in the harbor. I cannot blame her; she might have to leave in a hurry. But being beside her made it more convenient to get ashore. We moved out to the anchorage and tackled the Avon inflatable rubber dinghy for transportation ashore. These amazing "boats" are used throughout Europe. They are not popular in the United States, partly, undoubtedly, because of the different racing safety requirements. The Royal Ocean Racing Club allows the inflatable type for safety—kedging—equipment, while the Cruising Club of America requires a solid dinghy carried on deck for the same purposes.

It wasn't long before the various pieces were together and blown up. They make a very stable raft, with built-in fenders (the whole side) eliminating the "Don't bang the boat" and "Watch the paint" so often heard around U.S. waters. The freeboards aren't very high, and with any more than four persons, in a dinghy of the size *Rabbit* had, the trip could be a bit wet, especially if some motor boat happened to pass that kicked up a little wake.

Friday morning Dick and Mike were headed ashore to check out the arrival of our equipment. Mike had the dinghy alongside while Dick and I were still below. All of a sudden we saw, through the cabin window, two feet fly into the air. Simultaneously we heard a surprised "OH!" We were both on deck in a jiffy, just in time to see Mike pull himself out of the water over the dinghy's stern. He had jumped from *Rabbit*'s deck into the dinghy, planning to land evenly on both feet on the dinghy's bottom, thus avoiding the need to step on one side and the possibility of turning over. His landing was good, but with his weight too far aft the dinghy shot forward, resulting in his somersaulting over backward.

It was just what we needed. As Mike sheepishly crawled out of the water, Dick and I stood on deck laughing. That broke the tension and nervous excitement which had been building up within us.

Mike changed, and tried again. Dick wouldn't get into the dinghy until after Mike had done so safely. They made it ashore in one piece and dry. The fellow at the marine store wasn't in; neither were the items that had been ordered from London. He returned about an hour later, but without the charts, parallel rule, and dividers. We had given up on snap shackles. Time was too short to do anything now. We would have to settle for the borrowed chart we had used to cross over from Breskens, a small-scale chart showing the eastern approaches to the English Channel. It covered the entire area of the race, but didn't have some of the buoys in the channel off Harwich indicated by the course circular.

The fleet was heading for the starting area; ready or not, we saw that the moment of truth was approaching fast. Dick was surprised we didn't hear his heart pounding.

Our start, Class IIIb, was at 1345. The rest of the fleet was ahead of us, fighting its way out of Harwich in a 5-knot headwind and incoming tide. The #1 genoa was out of the bag for the first time; luckily it seemed to fit well. We were on the leeward end of the line and moving with clear air when our gun went. There was a crowd of boats at the windward end of the line, which had a better chance of fetching the first channel buoy about one mile distant than we did, but we were, we hoped, in less foul current. *Aladdin,* van de Stadt's Sprinter class, sailed by the notable Dutch designer himself, was to windward and moving well. She was a known rival. We rounded the first channel marker right in her wake. *Rabbit* was going well; the

Harwich–Hook of Holland Race

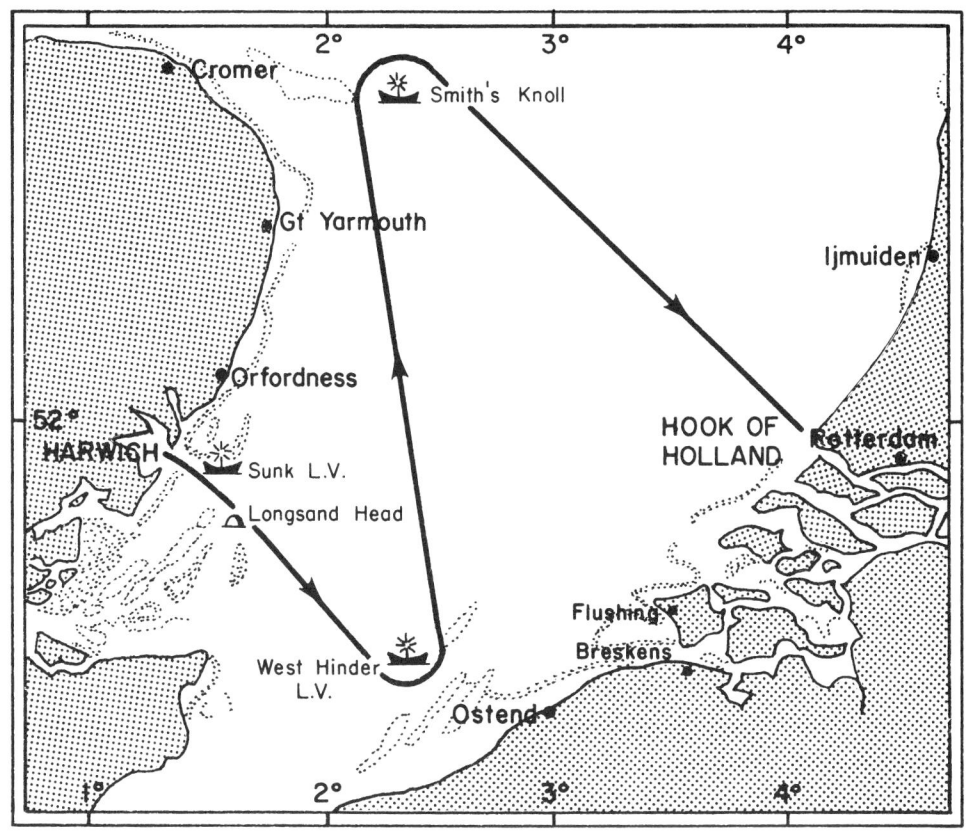

rest of Class IIIb was scattered out behind and we were quickly moving up with the stragglers from Class IIIa, who had started 15 minutes ahead of us. We followed the fleet out of Harwich on a very close reach, really footing, but not pointing as high as most of the fleet. Efficiency through hull speed seemed to compensate for their sideways slippage, for *Rabbit* did not fall off to leeward of them.

What a day to discover that one's first design could sail so well. The sun was out in full force, the wind at about 5 to 6 knots, and we were just able to lay our course to the first light vessel, West Hinder Light Ship, 80 miles away. Dick was overjoyed with *Rabbit*'s performance as we kept sliding past boats in Class IIIa; *Aladdin* had been left astern also. All afternoon the conditions remained the same; we just kept checking off the miles and boats we passed. An awesome feeling began to grow on us as bigger boats appeared ahead and slipped astern. Then, toward evening, *Hestia,* a Dutch sloop in Class IIIa, appeared abeam. Raced by the van Beuningen family, she is a legend in European waters for winning races. She had won her class in the last four North Sea Races and won overall three times. She was also a sure member of Holland's One Ton Cup team. Needless to say, we were overjoyed to see her abeam. As darkness fell and the tide changed, the wind dropped as well. Because of darkness and the concentration needed to keep *Rabbit* moving, we lost track of which lights belonged to *Hestia*. We changed back and forth from genoa to spinnaker, fighting to keep her going. The midnight to 4:00 A.M. watch was particularly long and tiring. *Rabbit* kept moving ahead all the time, but just barely.

Shortly after 5:00 A.M. we rounded the West Hinder Light Ship behind several Class II boats; *Hestia* was 10 minutes behind us. All day we fought our way north in light and spotty conditions, changing sails constantly. We continued to pass boats bigger than ourselves, boats with 30-foot waterlines and longer; *Rabbit*'s is only 24 feet! Only when the wind went to nil did the bigger, heavier, and deeper boats pull out on us. To our delight *Hestia* stayed in sight behind us all day. We caught *Firebrand,* a new Sparkman and Stephens boat and a top contender for the British Admiral's Cup team. *Tonnere de*

Breskens, the Dutch Admiral's Cup team member designed by Frans Maas, was seen. We were losing our sense of perspective.

Night again brought less wind and a good deal of slatting about, with constant work in an attempt to keep the sails drawing. It would have been nice to be moving faster, but at least the activity kept us warm. We were now feeling the effects of the North Sea, and even in June with little or no wind it was extremely cold. Luckily it wasn't a blustery northerly, for I hardly had the clothes to keep warm as it was.

As the sun rose early Sunday morning we converged on the Smith's Knoll Light Ship under spinnaker with a small patch of wind. Would it carry us around the Light Ship? We just made it before the wind changed. The tide turned west at the same time, leaving several boats unable to get around. *Hestia* had sneaked around ahead of us, 15 minutes earlier. Throughout the morning we held our position with her in a light southwest wind. During the afternoon the wind dropped again, leaving us unable to keep our spinnaker full due to the rolling of the boat and the lack of wind. *Hestia,* being just that much deeper, remained steadier in the water, keeping her spinnaker full, and became smaller and smaller as she drew ahead. Finding that we could carry the spinnaker further forward, we hardened up and headed southward. By evening *Hestia* was on the horizon abeam and ahead, heading toward the finish.

During the night the wind swung around, enabling us to head for where we thought the Hook of Holland to be. By daylight fog had descended on the coastline, making our approach a bit uncertain. Our limited navigational equipment and knowledge of the area were offset by the constant freighter traffic heading east. The only place safe for them to be going was the Hook of Holland on their way up river to Rotterdam. We followed them in, staying just north of the river's current as it flowed into the sea. There is a marked color difference as well as a difference in water movement. *Border Law,* an English Class I boat, followed us in.

We picked up the finish line and crossed at 0732 Monday morning, 3 hours behind *Hestia.* The big question was whether we should have stayed with her. They seemed to think so, as they apparently had a better breeze later.

We motored up the river to Rotterdam, escorted in real style by four British mine sweepers—we were completely unnoticed by them. Rotterdam Harbor covers many miles on both sides of the Rhine River where it passes Rotterdam, and continues downstream for quite a distance. There is much activity along both banks, with constant traffic moving up and down river. It is nearly as dangerous on a boat there as it is in a car in Paris.

We tied up at the Royal Maas Yacht Club and discovered that, out of 107 starters, we were the 11th boat to round the Smith's Knoll Light Ship and 11th to cross the finish line on a boat-for-boat basis. That wasn't bad, but on top of that we had given the fleet up to an hour's head start. On corrected time we finished second in Class III, behind *Hestia,* who had never seen another Class III boat after Smith's Knoll in all the years she has raced in the North Sea Race. Overall we finished third. Not bad for a boat that hadn't been released from the yard!

The rest of the day was spent straightening things up on board and relaxing, either sleeping or watching the fleet come in. As the afternoon wore on, we heard comments that we were being protested for not having an authorized bow pulpit, since it was located aft of the headstay. The result sheets in the club listed us as second in Class III. At about 1700 two Race Committee members came aboard for the "normal" inspection. (*Rabbit* had been measured in Holland, but not inspected with regard to meeting the safety regulations; this is done at the discretion of the Race Committee at any time they choose.) They made a thorough inspection, measuring the height of the lifelines in several different places, ensuring the proper stowage of chain, and so forth. The only comment that they made was that we should have a halyard for the racing flag so that it could be lowered when we were not racing. I had sewn ours to a metal flagstaff welded to the top of the mast about an hour before the race started. It served the dual purpose of a racing flag and wind pennant.

We felt better, for no mention was made of a protest or of the location of the bow pulpit.

A couple of hours later, as we crowded in to the prize-giving dinner, I happened to notice that *Rabbit* had been crossed off the result sheet and "disqualified" written in. Dick was able to speak to Alan Paul, the R.O.R.C. secretary, for a couple of minutes before the meal began. We had been disqualified for "having the bow pulpit halfway down the foredeck."

Dinner was good and there was plenty of wine, but those of us on *Rabbit* just weren't in the mood any longer. During the awards the commodore made several remarks about the "little boat *Rabbit*" which did very well, but was disqualified for incorrect placement of her lifelines. A great many people expressed disappointment at the way the disqualification was handled. Most were not convinced that our bow pulpit complied with the rule, but felt strongly that we should not have been thrown out of the race. Two courses of action had been open to the Race Committee: a warning to change the pulpit before the next race, and application of the usual 5% increase in time (this wouldn't have changed the final outcome at all).

We were none too happy about being disqualified, but to have it happen without a hearing or an attempt to notify us was unbelievable. The obstacles of campaigning with one's home base 3,000 miles away were large enough; to be treated this way as well was almost too much.

The Race Committee's contention was that the bow pulpit was unsafe, that Dick should have known about the meaning of the rule, that they had tried to contact him about it that afternoon, and that they were very sorry.

Dick and I met Lucas for supper at one of his favorite small eating establishments. He had located two hands to help us return to Breskens. Our route was to have been inland via the canals and rivers, but, because of the growing length of lists—to which had just been added a major project, "change bow pulpit"—and the short time before we had to get the boat to Cowes for our next race, we chose the offshore route. We left Rotterdam at 1:00 A.M. Wednesday to catch the tide down river. At the river mouth, with the tide ebbing and a strong west sou'wester (right on the nose) kicking up a short steep sea, I was reminded of the Buzzard's Bay entrance to the Cape Cod Canal during a sou'wester.

Setting the main and #2 genoa, we headed south along the coast. Our two Dutch friends, who came along because of their local knowledge, had never been down the coast, and retired to their bunks shortly after leaving the Hook of Holland. Dick and I navigated between buoys by watching for breaking seas which indicated the edge of the long shallow bar that follows the coast well offshore. We arrived in Breskens by early afternoon after a good sail.

Work on board commenced almost at once. Our lists were found and handed over to Peter, the competent yard foreman. The immediate problem was what to do with the bow pulpit in order to comply with the Race Committee's interpretation of their rule. There were two alternatives: to convert to a conventional pulpit, and give up the clean flow along the deck resulting from the sail's foot not having to rise up over the lifelines; or to come up with a method of keeping that clean flow along the deck. We decided to concentrate on a new method. We had to create and build a bow pulpit to encompass the forestay and still allow the genoa to be set outside of it and the lifelines. The practice common today of sheeting the genoa completely inside the lifelines had not then been adopted.

The solution, a combination of our ideas and the creative ability of the master welder at Maas' Yard, was anything but simple. The new pulpit took many shapes, changing this way and that way as the welder understood what we were trying to do; we appreciated the flexibility of welding. There was also the language problem, for we spoke no Dutch and the welder spoke very little English. But that wasn't as serious as it could have been in other circumstances; there seems to be an international understanding among perceptive craftsmen concerning their trade.

The pulpit which finally resulted was a three-legged affair, with the forward stanchion (or leg) an inch in front of the forestay and paral-

Redesigned bow pulpit with genoa attached outside it
Our redesigned bow pulpit (Below)

lel to it. The angle of this stanchion was the major change from a conventional pulpit. Normally, this stanchion is an extension of the bow's curve, thus extending from the stem fitting out in front of the boat. Tubing attached to the top of this stanchion leads back on either side of the foredeck to a set of stanchions and is then connected to the wire lifelines. Thus a railing is formed to help keep people on board. This requires that the headsails be hanked on inside the railing and led up over the lifelines to be sheeted in outside the lifelines. The result is a bad section of sail as it folds up over the lifeline, causing poor air flow, loss of valuable wind through the resulting hole, and an unesthetic-looking section in the otherwise perfectly set sail. One solution, of course, is to fasten the tack up off the deck high enough to allow the sail to clear the lifelines. This, though, leaves a much larger area through which valuable air is lost between the foot of the sail and the deck, and there is no allowance given in the rating rule for the distance off the deck of the foot of the headsail. Our ingenuity and persistence created a pulpit allowing the headsails to be set outside of it and flush with the deck, but also complying with the rule's interpretation that it should be forward of the headstay.

The new pulpit's forward stanchion was parallel to the forestay. The top railing of the pulpit formed a near-perfect V, with the apex welded to the top of the forward stanchion. The angle of the apex and the placement of the legs were critical. The pulpit had to be placed so that the headsails could be set either inside (conventionally) or outside of it without causing chafe or interference with the sails' set. The outside setting was primarily for the #1 genoa, which we expected to be able to carry in winds up to 10 knots. The #2 genoa was cut somewhat higher at the foot and when using this sail we weren't as concerned with the loss of some of the air. It could be attached either inside or outside, depending on the weather and the distance of the leg.

To set the headsails outside the pulpit the sail would be hanked on the forestay in the normal manner. The tack would go over the top of the pulpit and to leeward of it, then back to the snap shackle on the stem fitting. Thus the horizontal tubing of the pulpit was between the forestay and the luff of the sail. To tack with this arrangement, the snap shackle was opened, and the tack of the sail lifted up over the pulpit and pulled down outside the pulpit on the new leeward side to the snap shackle again.

One must remember here that *Rabbit* was designed for ocean racing, where one may tack only three or four times during a 300-mile race, and that the set of sails, air flow, and the never-ending problem of chafe should be of greater significance than tacking efficiency.

Saturday started slowly; no one was working in the yard. This was the first day of rest Dick had had in a long time. The months of anticipation, concern, worry, and decisions were over. It was as though the cards had all been dealt; what remained was just to play them as well as possible.

To play them that way we decided we had better do some sailing and find out what *Rabbit*'s likes were. A good opportunity was Sunday's around-the-buoy race at Ostend, 30 miles down the coast. After lunch we pushed off for Ostend, setting full sail, and headed into a 12-knot sou'wester. An hour and a half later *Rabbit* had chopped off about 100 yards of the total distance. The head wind and foul tide were too much for us. Dropping the genoa, we turned on the engine and powered into the wind and tide. Even though the engine was on full speed, we were just making headway. It wasn't long before Ostend was abandoned for a small harbor only 10 miles down the coast. As more time passed, the prospect of getting there looked poor as well, so we turned back, not to Breskens, but to Flushing, a harbor directly across the river from Breskens.

Sunday morning was spent inspecting the town and talking with some painting students from Amsterdam. One of them put our modern sailboat into his picture, tied up to the fishing fleet with the town behind.

Monday and Tuesday morning were allocated to completing the final touches before leaving the yard. Monday, activity started quickly: making changes here and there, fixing and adding things, applying a fresh coat of paint to the bottom, putting on the new propeller flown in from California. The biggest single project was still the bow pulpit.

Three changes were made as a result of our sailing Saturday. First, the tops of the aft stanchions were moved outboard 3 more inches. This allowed the sails to set better when attached inside the pulpit, but didn't hinder the sails' set when fastened outside. Two problems remained. The set of shackles and snap shackles required to give the tack a fair lead when set outside raised the foot of the sail some 6 to 7 inches above the deck. We were still dissatisfied; we wanted the foot flush with the deck. Also, I had found it rather clumsy unshackling the tack and reshackling it one-handed while trying to stay on deck with the tack jerking about. I hadn't even been in a hurry Saturday. These two problems were solved by the "rabbit ears"—stainless steel hooks welded to the outside of the stem fitting. They were open at the bottom to allow the tack cringle to slip over the end; with the sail pulled up, the tack would sit flush with the stem fitting and at deck level. Looking from leeward, one could see a clean marriage of hull and sail. A shock cord was to be used to keep the cringle from falling off the rabbit ear before the sail was hauled up tight. We discovered that this wasn't necessary; the cringle stayed on the ear, nearly always, of its own accord.

Even though progress was steadily being made in whittling down the size of the lists, we still weren't able to take our final departure from the yard Tuesday until after quitting time.

2. To Cowes

OUR intention was to catch the beginning of the westward-flowing tide at 3:00 P.M. out of Breskens, but we missed 2½ hours of it. With sails set we headed into a pleasant southwest wind. Conditions were the same as the previous Saturday, except for the direction of the tide. It took us about 30 minutes to reach the same location where we had turned back to Flushing after struggling for over 4 hours. I'm not sure I like all that tide. My home waters of Buzzard's Bay have enough tide to make racing interesting and tricky, but not enough to make it downright difficult to go sailing even with a good wind.

Our destination was Cowes, prior to Friday evening's start of the Morgan Cup Race off Portsmouth. With the wind from the southwest, it was going to be a beat for the 200-odd miles, making it a long trip. Adding to the length of the trip was the fact that there were only two of us on board, standing watches of 4 on and 4 off.

Just before sundown that first night out (Tuesday), and just after the tide changed, the wind petered out. The departure of the wind left us a long way from Cowes with an uncertain amount of fuel and a question as to which course to take. We could head for a harbor to refuel, wait for wind again, or power along hoping the wind would come in soon. There wasn't all the time in the world if we were to reach Cowes in time to unload some of our extra gear and stock up for the Morgan Cup Race. We gambled and decided to head for Cowes under power, hoping for wind soon.

The sou'wester returned within a couple of hours, requiring us to beat along the Dutch, Belgian, and French coast all night. We stayed inside the outer shallow sand bars, and early Wednesday morning beat past Dunkirk. With morning the wind increased continually. We rolled one reef in the main, and within the hour rolled in a second. Off Calais we had to decide whether to head on across the Channel for Dover or to put in to Calais. It was impossible to continue on in the lee of the French coast, because the coast takes a sharp curve to the south, leaving us on a lee shore as well as bringing us no closer to Cowes. The radio forecasts were predicting forces 6 to 7 in the Dover area.

We decided to proceed. I don't think there was much question really, but we reviewed the possibilities, as should be done under any circumstances. We were also pretty green—not in the gills, but on how *Rabbit* would handle in large seas. The stories of seas between Calais and Dover, especially with the tide against the wind (as it was), are something to scare even the calmest of people. But, with *Rabbit* designed and built to withstand worse than forces 6 to 7 off the Fastnet, and with daylight greatly reducing the danger of crossing the shipping lanes, we set across, exchanging the #2 genoa for the working jib first.

It turned out to be rather a pleasant crossing. Some of the time it was similar to a roller coaster ride—up and down. Some of the ups and downs were quicker and sharper than others, but the boat handled excellently. Thinking back on the crossing we realized to our pleasure that there had been no pounding as the bow fell off particularly sharp seas. This at least didn't tighten our nerves further, which were already wound up in anticipation of the coming campaign of three ocean races, the One Ton Cup (which had been added to our schedule), and Cowes Week.

The crossing may have been rougher than I recall, for I was off watch and slept nearly the whole way across. At least it wasn't rough enough to keep me from sleeping, although I was pretty tired by then. The two-day push to leave the yard, plus 20 hours of bashing to windward through a pitch-black night, 4 on, 4 off, had left neither of us very refreshed. It was a dismal moment each time to hear Dick's "Sandy, it's time." By working fast, and without being thrown across the cabin during an off-beat up or down, I was able to get "dressed" in five minutes, only to face four dull, cold, wet, and tiring hours on the helm.

The routine that developed for eating was somewhat unique, and stories about it seemed to spread quickly once we reached shore. We may have had something hot Tuesday night, or perhaps we even ate ashore early before leaving Breskens. But from then on, until we reached Cowes Thursday evening, the watch (of one person) just relieved would prepare chow: peanut butter and jam sandwiches. There was either strawberry or raspberry jam or orange marmalade. The "choice" depended on whichever jar was grabbed first.

Such a meal was tried once during the North Sea Race and met near-mutiny on the part of the Europeans on board. Mike was finally persuaded to try a peanut butter and jam sandwich; he even finished it, but said he'd never try it again. That was a strong statement for such a large and eager eater. The meal met similar success as the season progressed.

After reaching Cowes, we thought the menu amusing ourselves, and told prospective crew members about it to indicate our intention of racing to win. We weren't looking for just another pair of hands coming along for the ride.

Actually, peanut butter is one of the most nutritious foods known today. Dick's conclusion was that most of the time spent in preparing and eating food is wasted as far as winning the race is concerned. Energy is wasted preparing major meals and cleaning up afterward, and having a full, satisfied stomach is a great way to relax—just the opposite from what is wanted when racing. Dick is quick to point out that one maintains the competitive initiative best when well-nourished and well-rested. *Rabbit,* as well as his recent boats, has followed these theories.

By evening the wind had dropped to nothing, and we decided to gamble some more fuel away. Our landfall was 5 miles to the west of Dover. It wasn't worth the lost time to turn back to refuel there, so we crossed our fingers and powered on. Between 4:00 P.M. and 8:00 P.M. I was on watch. A southerly came up strong enough for us to make ground against the tide. Then it swung into the southeast and east, steadily increasing in velocity all the time. With the full main and #2 genoa up, *Rabbit* began to reel off the miles along the coast. The wind didn't stop in the east, but continued into the northeast. Then it began to rain. I cannot really call it just rain; the drops were the size of large marbles. As they were being driven by 20 knots of wind, they were impossible to face. Luckily we were going with the wind. Even with the hatch cover pulled closed, Dick had to remain in the middle of the cabin to keep from getting soaked.

What a ride! Oh to have the spinnaker up, for *Rabbit* really loved this. Maybe we would get a good tough run back from Fastnet Rock.

I must have been relieved again and gone to sleep, for the next thing I recall is that we were once again hard on the wind, which was now out of the northwest at about 25 knots. It was pitch black out, and the light on Beachy Head was off the starboard bow. I'm not sure I really woke up for an hour after changing watch. Beachy Head Light had gotten brighter, quite close abeam. I did wake up when a fishing trawler, well lit up, passed between us and the light with no concern at all. I couldn't believe it. I'd been subconsciously listening for breakers on the rocks beneath the light. I had even considered tacking offshore for a while, but knew we wanted to get into the bay and out of as much foul tide as possible, so I had been hanging on. After being fully awakened by the trawler, I investigated what was ahead of us. I had finally considered us past Beachy Head Light and was looking for my next point of interest. There were two sets of lights well ahead, just under the genoa, indicating two towns. I recalled seeing on the chart one town which had a small harbor and another which didn't. I settled back down to sailing, expecting to see them emerge behind the genoa shortly.

The wind was still blowing and we were hard on the wind, moving through the water very well. But we just couldn't get past that light on Beachy Head. Suddenly one of those towns came steaming past on the way out to the fishing grounds. The other remained where it had previously been.

I must have begun to mutter, for Dick appeared in the companionway and asked "How's it going?" I hope I answered him civilly, but I wasn't feeling that way—Beachy Head Light was still abeam. He acknowledged that the tide flowed pretty strongly around this headland and that it was at its maximum against us. For some reason he decided to turn the radio on. After about two minutes of rock-and-roll one of the songs was interrupted by the disc jockey with "We interrupt this program to bring you a weather bulletin." For the area we were in, the forecast was for westerly winds at force 8 (gale) and force 9 (strong gale) for the remainder of the night. Following that news the rock-and-roll continued, but on *Rabbit* we turned it off.

I'm not sure how much sleep Dick got when off watch. He was in his bunk with eyes closed, but I don't think he was asleep much of the time. The wheels wouldn't stop turning to allow him the rest he needed. I know I was tired, even though I got 3½ hours sleep out of every 8. My temper was deteriorating with Beachy Head Light glued to our starboard beam. By now I'd changed the name of this prominent light to Bitchy Head; I was not in a good mood.

When Dick suggested that we might ride things out in New Haven (the town with a harbor I had seen ahead—it was still there, the bearing unchanged), I wasn't opposed in the slightest, as long as we got away from Beachy Head.

On went the good old engine with an unknown quantity of fuel. Our rough calculations indicated there was ample fuel to get us to New Haven. The problem would arise if we had to power much of the way to Cowes without refueling.

It seemed like hours that we powered and sailed for New Haven. Actually, it couldn't have been too long, for the watch hadn't changed. But Beachy Head was still abeam. We gave up the fight for New Haven, having gained nothing. So with the working jib and reefed main we tacked out into the Channel and prepared ourselves for whatever might be unleashed at us.

Fortunately, the gales never came. Even so, it had been a long and bitterly tiring night for both of us. By mid-morning we changed back to the #2 genoa and tacked back for the English coast, having little idea where we would be upon sighting land. To our great surprise and delight our landfall was the Nab Tower off Portsmouth. Two hours later we were tied up in the trots at Cowes.

There was no relaxing the next morning. Somehow there were always things to do or get. One of the important tasks was for us to be entered in the race. It turned out that the R.O.R.C. had set up their offices in Portsmouth rather than in Cowes. (They never have had the Morgan Cup Race headquarters in Cowes, but Cowes is the central location for all racing as far as we foreigners are concerned.) It wouldn't have mattered had we known. Dick's brother John was joining us for this race, and it had been prearranged that he would meet us in Cowes that afternoon. We also wanted to leave off the special One Ton Cup mainsail and boom in Cowes.

At the moment there were just the three of us for the race. Dick's call to the R.O.R.C. office in Portsmouth alerted them to our need of crew. They said that we were entered in the race and to stop by to pick up the race circulars any time before the start.

John arrived on board at 3:30. We had found no one at Cowes able to join us, and so pushed off for Portsmouth. The wind was whooping along the Solent at 30 knots plus, out of the southwest. We weren't looking for too much excitement yet, and therefore only set the working jib. Under this alone, *Rabbit* ran along between 7 and 8 knots.

In Portsmouth Dick jumped ship to check in with the Race Committee. We hoped there would be some available crew looking for a berth. He was back, alone, in a matter of minutes. Several boats had just withdrawn from the race and we certainly could pirate some of their crews, if we could find them. We didn't have much time to look; the race was about to begin. One swing past the Camper and Nicholson Yard, where there wasn't a soul around, and just the three of us headed for the start.

Off Portsmouth the wind was still blowing 30 m.p.h. from the southwest. The starting area was a mass of confusion. The line, a transit on shore, was difficult to locate, and the water was in a turmoil from tide, wind, and the wakes from so many boats. We finally started, under working jib and well-reefed main. The fleet reached out past the forts and then hardened onto the wind. It wasn't long before we set up a watch system: 2 hours on, 4 hours off. I think something was mentioned about the person who had just been relieved being the one to call for any assistance, or maybe it was the one to come on watch next. Whichever it was, it didn't work out.

In fact, no change of sail was made except during a watch change.

Rabbit *at the start of the Morgan Cup race*

Morgan Cup Race

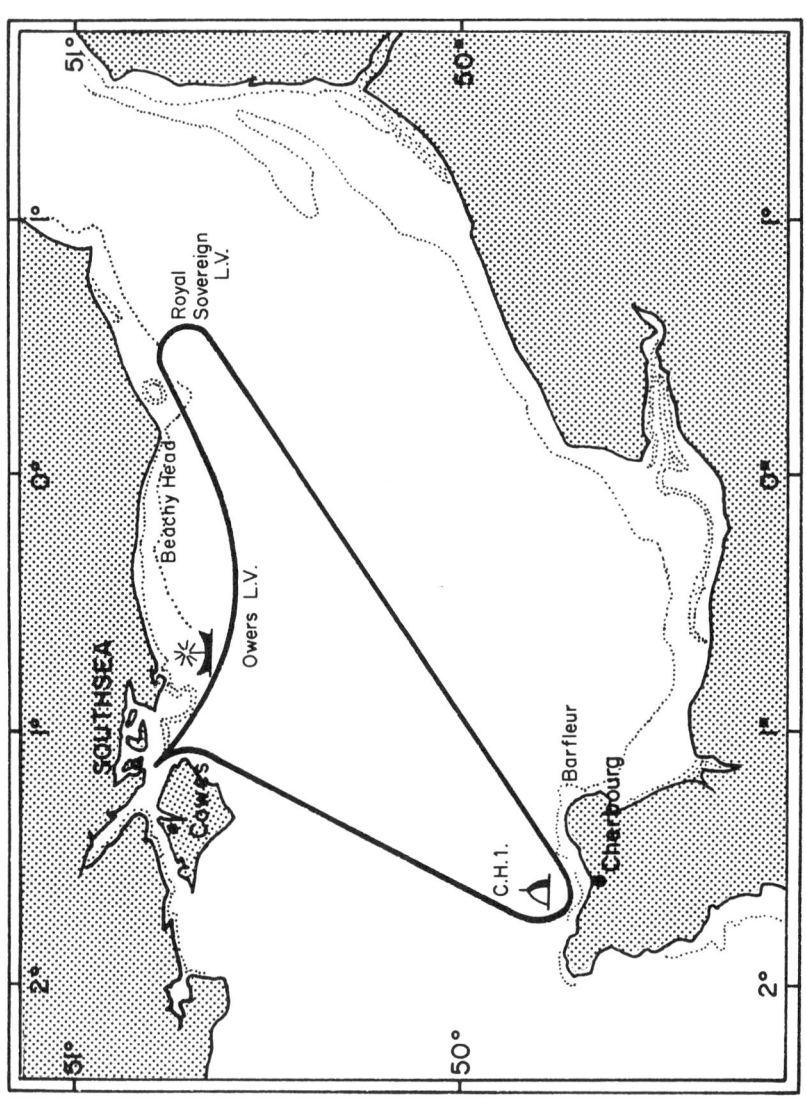

We were functioning in low gear, and it took the new watch about an hour to digest the situation. By then, no one wanted to call anyone out of his bunk during the middle of the watch; besides, it was always "right on the edge" for a different sail, and the conditions might have changed back any minute.

Our jib and reefed main was the appropriate rig for the start, where we felt the full weight of the southwest wind funnelling down the Solent. But once outside the Solent where the true sou'wester was blowing, we were under-canvassed. Being tired and short-handed we were always slow to add more sail throughout the night as the wind diminished. At dawn we found ourselves off the French coast, about 20 miles to leeward of our mark. The wind, having swung into the west, had dropped to about 5 m.p.h. It took several hours of hard sailing without gaining on the shore for us to appreciate the strength of the tide. Some 4 hours of head tide were yet to come, so we went in to the shore, out of the strongest tide. It was one of those beautiful clear mornings when it is a pleasure to be on the water. We were between the sun and shore, and thus able to spot easily the rock piles indicated on the chart that lie just below the surface. Otherwise there was plenty of water, and we began to work along in close to shore. This was the first time we had actually done any tacking with the #1 genoa and the rabbit ears. At first we tried it with one person working the halyard, another changing the tack over, and the third handling the sheets and steering. This was soon changed to one person on the foredeck handling the loosening of the halyard and changing the tack. Two people on the foredeck put too much weight forward, especially with only one person's weight offsetting it aft. The task aft was more than one person could readily handle.

We weren't too depressed at first light that morning. We realized that we had not been too sharp during the crossing, and, although none of the real competitors we would have liked to have seen were around, there were quite a few boats, even some Class II, in sight. One of these followed us in toward the French shore. She stayed about a mile off, while we went in close. We found later that the crew from this boat was immensely impressed by how close we went in. They were more interested, though, in the gymnastics that I went through on the foredeck each time we tacked. It was the first time anyone had seen the new system in operation.

We rounded Cherbourg #1 at 1610 with several other boats. Unfortunately, we had seen a long procession of spinnakers all afternoon, heading for the next mark: Royal Sovereign Light Ship, located off my friend, Beachy Head.

For the remainder of the afternoon and throughout the night the apparent wind was just enough to keep us moving over the bottom. The apparent wind speed would increase as we fought against the tide and would drop when the tide was in our favor. It was a frustrating night keeping the spinnaker full and the boat moving. By morning we were still some 40 miles from the Royal Sovereign. The discouraging part of it was that the weather remained the same, with no change visible in the near future.

The noon shipping forecast (weather report for the whole area surrounding England) discouraged us further; more of the same with no change in sight for at least 24 hours. The crowning blow was the report that the Royal Sovereign had a gentle land breeze. This meant of course that the lead boats were marching along, widening still further the already large gap between them and ourselves.

So, with over 100 miles to the finish, the prospect of covering the distance within a reasonable time frame looked very dubious. As we would be bringing up the rear of the fleet to boot, we chose to retire from the race. We headed for Cowes on a broad reach, picking up a pleasant breeze as we closed with land.

Clarion of Wight (Class II) received a start when she saw us approach the forts off Portsmouth right behind her. She crossed the finish line. We dropped sails and powered past the finish line and on to Cowes. The wind dropped completely, making it look doubtful that anyone would finish for a long, long time.

Any remaining regrets on our withdrawing from the race disappeared completely as we sat in the Gloucester Hotel eating dinner. The Solent's surface looked like a sheet of glass. It stayed that way through Monday noon, when a slight breeze finally came in.

Those Class III boats that stuck it out started finishing Monday evening. The last boat to finish didn't get in until well into Tuesday.

We had one more race for tuning, the Cowes-Dinard Race, before the serious competition of the One Ton Cup and Cowes Week. In the very light wind we were caught well behind the line as our starting gun was fired. With clear air and our 900-square-foot light spinnaker up we slowly gained on our class. Off the forts we were up with the class leaders. Upon hardening up for the Nab Tower we took two successive knockdowns. They weren't particularly dramatic; we just lost steerage and rounded up. On the third knockdown, the snap shackle on the spinnaker sheet snapped open. It was obviously time for the genoa, so up it went.

I'm told I was handling the foredeck. I cannot believe it, but apparently, with the intention of getting the spinnaker down quickly, I let the spinnaker go adrift from the pole and guy. There we were, reaching along with the genoa up and the spinnaker floating off to leeward, attached to us only at the top of the mast. Sailing off before the wind, we tried all sorts of maneuvers to retrieve the spinnaker. As we struggled on, falling further and further to leeward, the fleet sailed by on its way to the Nab Tower. Finally we were able to blanket the spinnaker behind main and genoa, which enabled us to catch up with it and haul it back to the deck. It was quickly disposed of below decks, where we hoped it would cause us no further troubles, and we returned to the race.

With four on board for this race, and all of us relatively well rested, we were able to perform the sail changes throughout the night with some manner of efficiency and proper timing. By morning, we were off Cherbourg. Quite a number of boats were in sight, either Class I or Class III. What had happened to the Class II boats? Once again the wind was light from the southwest and the tide against us. This was made worse by the current flowing to the northeast through Alderney Race at anywhere up to 6 knots.

We rounded the Casquets at about 1700, and, in a 12-knot breeze, reached along for the finish. *Drumbeat* and *Rimrod* were offshore of us, and four Class II boats were in sight behind. Although we were going well, the longer water lines of the Class I and II boats were too much for us, and our pursuers started to bear down on us. Shortly after 2000 we decided to try our reaching spinnaker in an effort to stay ahead of them.

They were apparently happy with their rigs, for there was no activity on any of them—until we started to pull away from them with our spinnaker up. Heads popped up from below to watch our progress. Then, one by one, each crew prepared its own spinnaker gear; none was ever raised. The wind pulled ahead, forcing us to bear off well below our desired course. The crews behind us settled down to normalcy again, with the off watch going back to their interrupted dinner. We returned to our course under genoa. It was a worthwhile try, and amused us by the concern it caused the boats overtaking us.

In the light breeze off Dinard, the incoming tide nearly drew us past the finish line, even after we had seen two boats just ahead of us beating up to the line on the opposite tack. We too had to tack to cross the line. The strong tides off Dinard make the finish of this race a bit tense at times, especially when accompanied by light winds.

We were just in time to catch the first group of racers to pass through the locks into St. Malo. The great basin is right near the center of town, unaffected by the 30-to-40-foot rise and fall of tide. With the locks open for only an hour and a half before and after each high water, the change in water level inside the basin is next to nothing. The whole basin gets flushed out several times each year.

The winner, *Alcatraz,* a Class III boat, was a member of the French One Ton Cup team. We finished fourth on corrected time. Not bad. Maybe *Rabbit* was a pretty fast boat after all, we thought—when sailed properly. If we could only get tuned up in time, we would find out during the One Ton Cup.

Cowes–Dinard Race

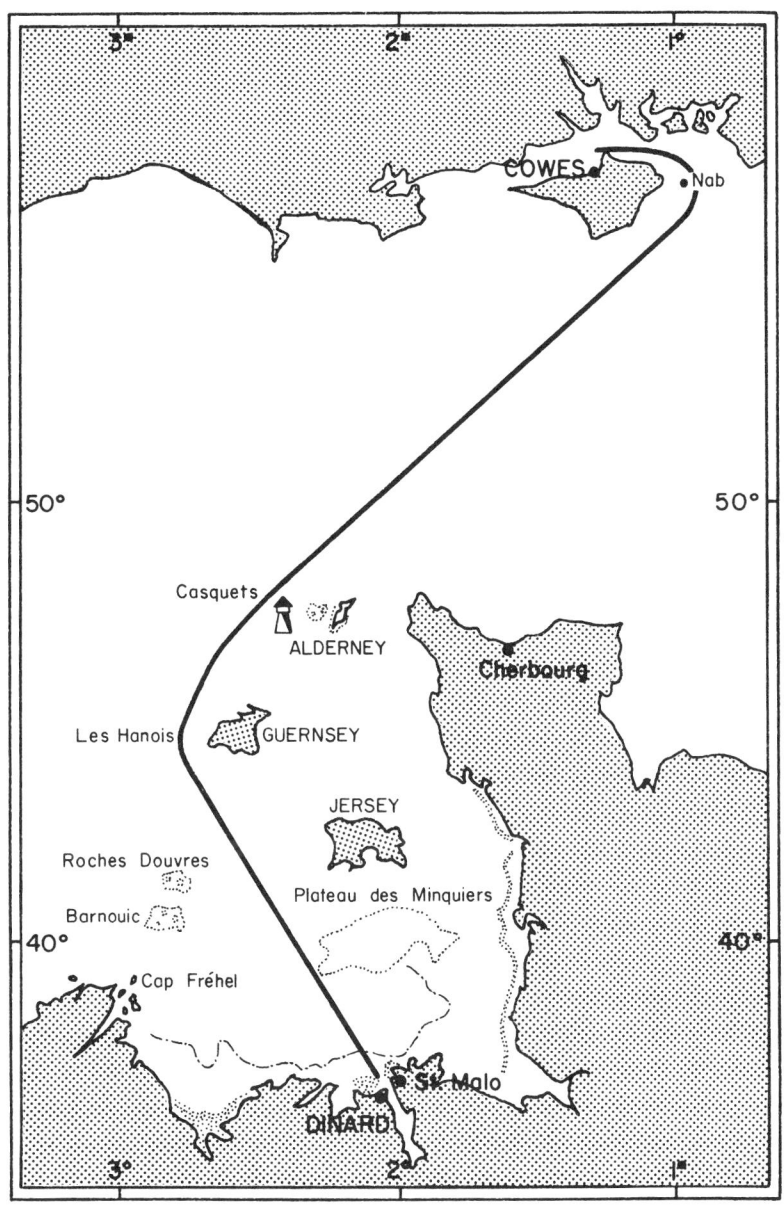

3. Dinard to Le Havre

IN designing *Rabbit,* Dick had been extremely concerned with laying out the interior so that she would not be considered a stripped-out racing machine. Most people, upon first going below on *Rabbit,* were amazed at the amount of room and light there was. The spaciousness of the cabin was a result of the boat's beam, the use of steel construction, and an unusually large amount of light. The steel ribs required are appreciably smaller than those on a wooden boat of comparable size. The effective width below is from the inside of the ribs rather than from the hull itself. The light was provided through three large plexiglass windows mounted on each side of the cabin trunk. The typical European boat was much narrower and was fitted out with more heavy-looking fixtures below decks. Many of the reporters, upon seeing *Rabbit* below decks, recognized the difference. And many of them, though not understanding why there was a difference, referred to *Rabbit* as strictly a racing boat.

Rabbit was actually a cruising boat, providing all the comfort and ease of handling one could desire. For the sail to Le Havre, where the One Ton Cup was to be held, Dick's wife and two children joined us.

Our departure from St. Malo, one morning, was in company with *Myth of Malham.* (She was designed by John Illingworth twenty years ago as a rule beater and was the first "small" boat to enter ocean racing. Even today, she does very well against the modern rule beaters.) The marine artist and sailor Marin Marie, sailing *Myth,* guided us into Isles Chausey. As we left St. Malo, *Alcatraz* was also in company with us. She hoisted her spinnaker and we followed suit; *Myth* didn't bother. She wasn't going to be lured into a race. Much to our delight, we pulled away from both *Myth* and *Alcatraz.* This slight encounter raised our hopes for the upcoming One Ton Cup.

We sailed in the narrow entrance to Chausey at nearly low water and tied up alongside *Drumbeat* and *Greenfly.* Isles Chausey is interesting. At low water, land is the predominating feature in a vast area of islands, weed-covered rocks, and sandy beaches, separated by narrow channels and ponds of water. At high water, due to the tre-

Channel Islands

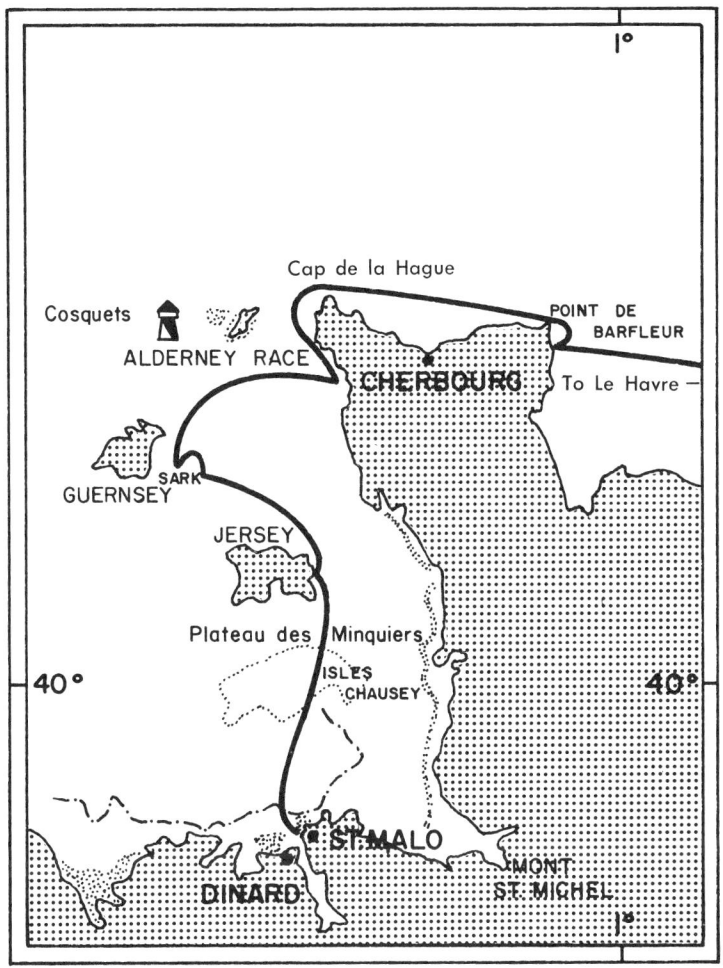

mendous range of tide (30 to 40 feet), the area takes the form of a group of islands and rocks rising from the sea. The scene is changing constantly.

The island group measures some 6 miles by 2½. Grande Isle, the largest and only populated island, is less than a mile long with four sandy bays between five pronounced headlands. The permanent population numbers approximately 40, with their livelihood centered around fishing. During the summer, the population increases and the island is invaded by tourists who keep the two small hotels active. We joined this latter group and put ashore.

Adlard Coles writes in his book *Channel Harbours and Anchorages,* "Many yachtsmen have cast wistful eyes in the direction of the 'Mount' (Mont St. Michel), for on the chart it does not look difficult of access on a high Spring tide. Nevertheless, it is said that the tide runs at the speed of galloping horses. There are quicksands, and if by chance the yacht ran aground she might never lift again, since the suction on the keel might hold her in deadly embrace. There are also fish stakes in various unspecified parts of the bay." From the distance, the Mount looks like an anchored battleship. Once it was an old fortress and state prison, but it has been turned into an abbey. Now it is one of the great monuments of France.

We joined the many sailors in casting a wistful eye toward the Mount. The tides were just right to get in and out the next day. Adlard Coles' warnings of the dangers were surely overexaggerated by years and years of stories. We didn't overlook the fact that the trip wasn't without its dangers, but if one kept one's head and picked good conditions it certainly could be undertaken successfully. In addition, *Rabbit* was a shallow draft boat.

The next morning, though, we departed from Isles Chausey via the north channel, wiggling through the rock outcrops. With spinnaker set we headed north, leaving Mont St. Michel for another time. By mid-morning our course converged with that of *Pen Duick II*. We had a "race" with her in the light winds, changing to the #1 genoa as the wind pulled ahead. Early in the afternoon, with *Pen Duick II* just ahead of us, the wind went flat. We turned on our mechanical wind and powered into the tide. *Pen Duick II* was left behind, for she is truly a sailing boat and has no engine.

Fortunately we were approaching the island of Jersey as fog descended over the land. Navigating in this area during storms or fog must be extremely difficult. The very strong tides, with their many countercurrents and eddies, and the very few navigational aids, make it difficult even in clear weather. Just imagine the challenge of a race through the area.

Our luck enabled us to follow the shore to St. Catherine's Bay, where we picked up a mooring behind the long breakwater extending from shore to the north. This provided ample shelter from any winds west of north and south. Soon after we had settled down, a lad came alongside in a motor boat. He requested that we anchor a little way off. We had picked up a race buoy that wouldn't hold us—and that they were about to use. He showed us where to anchor, and as we ate supper we watched the dinghies racing around the buoy we had just left.

Early the next morning we sailed from St. Catherine's Bay with an overcast sky and head winds, but made good time with a favorable tide. Our plan was to stop for lunch in Creux Harbor on the east coast of Sark Island and then spend the night in St. Peter Port on Guernsey, 8 miles west of Sark. After investigating the coastal guide we changed our plans, for Creux Harbor dries out at low water, which was at noon that day.

Instead we sailed around the northern end of Sark and south along the west coast, passing through the narrow Gauliot Pass, only 80 yards wide. The pass is a clean-cut gash between two islands, with cliffs so high that coastal steamers easily pass underneath the telephone wires which stretch across it. The water has a reputed speed of 10 knots during springs. We entered at low water and the wild tide and overfalls were non-existent. We anchored in a deep cove which opens just south of the pass.

We spent such a long time walking around Sark that we didn't return to *Rabbit* until late. The cove was well protected from the northeast wind that was blowing, so we stayed put for the night.

Our departure the next morning was delayed to coincide with a fair tide. Even though we were beating into a 10-to-20-knot nor'easter we made great time over the bottom. But it wasn't good enough to get us through Alderney Race before the tide turned against us. Alderney Race commands a great deal of respect. The current races through there at speeds up to 9 knots. One couldn't help but dream of being under spinnaker in a strong sou'wester, moving through the water at 9 or 10 knots, in addition to a favorable current of another 9 knots. Moving at 18 knots over the bottom, we would probably be through before we realized the thrill of it.

In reality both wind and tide were against us when we reached the Race, so there was no sense in even trying. Instead we headed for cover under the southwest corner of the Cherbourg Peninsula. Our plan was to wait for the change of tide under Cap de la Hague. Further reading in the coastal guide indicated that the town of Dielette could offer us a chance to stop and stretch our legs ashore, so we changed our course for it. We anchored off the breakwater, for it was low water and the artificial harbor had dried out. Most of the small harbors along this coast do dry out at low water. They provide protection for the small fishing dories and for those boats which have "legs." These legs are beams, attached to either side of the hull, which are the same depth as the keel. Thus the boat sits on its keel, with the legs to keep the boat from tipping over onto its side.

Our anchorage would have been uncomfortable had the wind had any westerly to it. It was still out of the northeast, coming right offshore and providing a perfect protection.

With evening approaching, we weighed anchor and powered along the beach. It looked like beautiful sand, but undoubtedly was well-rounded stones. We were headed for the cliffs of Cap de la Hague, right around the corner from the Race.

Our stomachs began protesting well before we reached our proposed anchorage. Off the very attractive little village of Vauville we decided to go ashore for supper. With the tide rising, we moved into about 10 feet of water and anchored. There was no thought of a harbor, just a long open beach. The wind was still offshore, and we lay as protected and comfortable as if we had been in a cosy land-locked harbor somewhere.

It was a beautiful evening as we rowed ashore in the rubber dinghy, dressed in our complete foul weather gear. The reason for all the gear was the few minutes involved in landing. The prevailing southwest swells were still around, though they were only noticeable where they were breaking as they rolled up the stony resistance. This was going to call for some fancy footwork and timing to get in without getting wet. We would have to wait for a swell to carry us in as far as we could go, then jump out and get up the beach—without leaving the dinghy behind or letting it be carried back with the receding water. We made it, without getting more than one foot wet. We would be hard pressed to duplicate our landing success when launching.

It was late by the time we started looking for a place to eat. The only café wasn't open, but there was another café up the road, so we started walking. Before we left the village, though, we met two girls. They asked if we were looking for something, as they had seen us come ashore. It turned out that the nearest café was 3 or 4 kilometers up the road, a distance we had no intention of walking. As we were saying good-bye, one of the girls produced a dozen fresh eggs. We thanked them and headed back to the boat for supper.

The launching of the rubber dinghy with us all on board was quite an experience. Dick's wife took charge of the eggs while Dick and I handled the dinghy. With one of us on each side, we waited for a good chance. The plan of attack was to move down the beach with the receding water. At the water's lowest point we would push the dinghy out into the water as far as possible, jump on board, and paddle off before the next wave could take us back up the beach and leave us high and dry. We took a couple of false starts and then made it. There wasn't even an egg broken as we landed helter-skelter in and on the dinghy. That night we simply moved into a little deeper water and anchored.

The wind was still northeast as we got under way the next morning. Just as the anchor was stowed, though, the engine stopped. It stopped in that unmistakable way an engine does when the gas tank goes dry. But it was no problem: up with the sails, and the tide carried us to windward and through Alderney Race in no time at all. As the day wore on the wind swung to the north, enabling us to reach along the northern coast of the peninsula toward Barfleur. It was a beautiful day, with a nice breeze for quiet sailing; everyone was enjoying himself. We debated briefly on going into Cherbourg for gas, but the complications outweighed the immediate need, as we were currently making good progress.

As we approached Pointe de Barfleur, the tide began to turn against us, and the wind died as it swung further to the west. The chart indicates very shallow water, extending 3 or 4 miles off the point, that turns into a dangerous race as the current builds up speed around the point. We approached Barfleur right along the coast, going in until we saw bottom, in order to stay out of the adverse tide as much as possible. Under the light we found ourselves in a counter-current that drew us right along. The chart indicates an inner passage very close to land, almost underneath the light. But we couldn't find it listed as a possible passage in any of the navigational guide books we had. Nonetheless, we decided to go through. The conditions were just right for it, with the sun at our backs making visibility very good, a light wind, and the tide not yet strong. We would never have made it out around the race with the present wind and increasing tide.

The local fishermen must use it on good days, for there is a pole on the shore side of the passage. Depending on the tide and wind conditions, the passage is some 40 yards wide. We could see the race building to port and the shallows to starboard. We approached under main very slowly, partly due to the very light wind which was dead astern and partly due to an obvious need for caution. It looked as if we had it made as the pole inched its way abeam, with open calm water just ahead. But then we began to lose ground on the pole! As we looked back on either side of the passage, the overfalls where the counter-current met the true current looked rough and nasty. We wanted no part of them. The genoa was up and wung out in record time. We had several anxious minutes, for if we didn't make it there would be trouble going back. The greatly added sail area of the genoa was just enough to do the trick, and we sneaked through the passage into safe water. We wondered whether Adlard Coles knew of this passage.

Anchored off Barfleur Harbor—it also dries out at low water—we immediately set about transferring gas out to the boat in a plastic jerry can. Our next day's passage had to be the 60-odd miles across to Le Havre. The bay is noted for its light winds. We weren't anxious to be left sitting in the middle with no wind or fuel. Our fuel consumption calculations indicated that, with both gas tank and jerry can full, we would run out just off Le Havre should we have to power the whole distance.

Sunday was spent sailing and motoring to Le Havre. It was a day of calm and relaxation before the storm. The storm this time would be the preparations for the first One Ton Cup.

Rabbit, *with One Ton main and with the genoa hanked on outside the bow pulpit*

4. First One Ton Cup

ALL participants were required to report no later than Monday morning for their boats to be checked, sails measured, and ratings verified. Fourteen boats and crews gathered at the Yacht Basin in Le Havre. Eight countries were represented, three of which had held trials in order to select their teams. France, England, and Holland were represented by three boats each; the remaining countries, Denmark, Sweden, Germany, Belgium, and the United States, were represented by one each.

The One Ton Cup is an historic trophy that has been in competition since 1898. The name refers to the first class that competed for it when several members of the Cercle de la Voile de Paris gave it for international competition. Since then it has been sailed for almost continuously, except during wartime, with the bulk of the competition having been sailed in 6-meters.

When the 6-meter class went into a decline in recent years, C.V.P. members, led by Jean Peytel, wondered how to give this large and splendid trophy new life. They realized that offshore racing had overwhelmed round-the-buoy keelboat racing in popularity. Early in 1965 they decided to give it to ocean racing boats, on the condition that they race without handicaps or time allowances, in a series of short and long races. All competitors must rate no more than 22 feet R.O.R.C. measurement rule and fit the accommodation requirements of the I.Y.R.U. 8-meter cruiser/racer class.

Countries are invited to enter up to three boats. Each boat is scored individually, not as a team, with the long races counting double. The boat with the highest score wins the trophy and her Yacht Club has the privilege of sponsoring the next series.

This was to turn into a truly unique series of races. The plans hadn't been completed in sufficient time to enable people to take full advantage of the requirements, even though the concept had immediate and widespread appeal. There just wasn't time to design, build, and tune a new boat that rated exactly 22.0 feet, incorporating all of the latest in design.

Many people thought that *Rabbit* had been designed with this series especially in mind. She undoubtedly would have been had her plans been completed after those for this series. Her regular R.O.R.C. rating was actually 20.34 feet, over a foot and a half below the rating stipulated for this series. In an attempt to compensate for this lower rating we replaced the regular mainsail with one 6 feet longer along the foot. This increased the main by 30%, giving us, we hoped, great sail power in light air and when reaching or running. Under the R.O.R.C. rules, anything over 150% overlap of the genoa is penalized. *Rabbit* already had a 180% overlapping genoa and there seemed to be no practical way to increase the sail area in the foretriangle. The "One Ton" main increased our rating to 21.3 feet. What else could we do to make the boat go faster as long as it didn't raise the rating more than an additional .7 of a foot? We thought of removing the propeller. This would raise the rating up to 21.7 feet. However, the difficulty of removing the propeller and the minimum amount of drag and turbulence it caused overrode any advantage of racing without it.

The boats gathered for this series were both new and old. The vast majority of them were well proven boats which had to be changed in order to comply with the 8-meter accommodation requirements or to adjust their rating to 22 feet or just below it. Cabin tops had to be lengthened, cabin soles had to be increased, water tanks and/or gas tanks were added especially for this series. The owners and crews were keen on doing everything possible to hit 22.0 feet exactly.

The organizers and measurers made a determined effort to insure that each boat complied with the rules. They also realized this was the first go-round for everyone and were lenient in interpreting some of the rules. We had to increase our water capacity, and were fortunate to find and "install" at the last minute a suitable container, although it was hardly functional, having recently been a gas tank.

There was a generally friendly interchange of ideas and investigation of each boat and its equipment as we prepared for the racing. We met nothing but complete cooperation and a genuine desire to help from all the merchants we came in contact with, regardless of our needs.

Even so, we felt at a disadvantage. Our home base was some 3,000 miles across an ocean. The other boats had their total resources within a stone's throw, either across the Channel or along this coast. The feeling of isolation didn't remain long, for the New York dock strike was in progress, leaving little to keep Edward Stettinius, an American, at his work for the U.S. Shipping Lines in Le Havre. Being interested in sailing, he appeared at the Yacht Club and offered us his assistance. This reassured us greatly; we now had his knowledge of the area and the resources to get things done should an emergency arise. Another psychological boost was some advanced detailed weather information provided through the U.S. Lines.

The first race, a 30-miler, started in a fresh southwest breeze. The course was a close reach bearing around a buoy into a spinnaker run, then a long windward leg, and a run to the finish. The start was good all along the line. We were in good position with clear air. With the big #1 genoa and the extra big main we really revelled in the conditions. The wind for this angle of sailing was just the strength we could handle. Had we been required to harden onto the wind we would have had too much sail up.

As we approached the first buoy it was nip and tuck whether we could pull ahead of *Alcatraz* to lead the fleet around. We arrived first and got the spinnaker flying immediately. I don't know how that happened, for I was continually getting something twisted. Maybe it was Dick's persistence; I think he asked me eight times if everything was clear and ready as we approached the mark. During the run we opened out a little on the fleet, carrying our spinnaker closer to the leeward mark than our pursuers. Once again the sail handling was completed without a tangle as we hardened onto the wind.

We felt pleased that we were competitive with the fleet as long as the wind didn't increase, and we continued the superb sail handling. *Alcatraz, Ilex II,* and *Aladdin* rounded right behind us and slowly worked to windward. *Hestia*, having started poorly, was well back at the leeward mark. She split tacks and led a contingent to the south.

Shortly, however, the weather went haywire. The wind was light and from all over the compass. Thunderstorms continually moved over the fleet. Hardly any wind came with them; it just changed direction as the storm moved through. Sail changes were continuous as the fleet spread out over the bay. We stayed pretty much on the rhumb line, and were actually farther offshore than most of the fleet. The inshore contingent, still led by *Hestia,* picked up a southerly and carried spinnakers to the erstwhile weather mark. *Hestia* rounded this mark a mile ahead of everyone else. Soon after, the wind obligingly changed once again so that she hoisted her spinnaker and ran in to the finish off Le Havre.

We beat up to the mark, and were just able to round it as a storm passed overhead. As the storm went by we very slowly continued, under spinnaker and with the tide, toward the finish. *Ilex* and *Diana* were right with us at the mark, but were unable to carry the slight breeze around. They had to anchor and wait for another storm. It was a long run back to the finish, with the pole sometimes on the forestay and sometimes squared away. We finished fifth behind *Hestia, Aladdin, Giraglia,* and *Alcatraz* at 7:00 P.M. after a long hard day. Nearly 10 hours of high-geared concentration and innumerable sail changes left us exhausted.

The start of the ocean race was the next afternoon. The first mark was CH 1 off Cherbourg, then around the Nab Tower and back across the Channel to finish off Le Havre. An addition to the course came out that evening: we were to mind the buoy off Barfleur Light. This was an amusing addition for we had used some gamesmanship upon arriving in Le Havre. Dick had mentioned to Adlard Coles, in a group, that we had found this passage inside the Barfleur Race. Dick was speculating that this could be a fine place to go if the wind were light and we were fighting the tide. Joining in on the game, Adlard Coles said he knew of the passage and speculated right along with Dick about using it. The thought of this possible shortcut threw the rest of the racers way off balance. The Committee, knowing that the area can be extremely dangerous, added the mark to our course to prevent any recklessness.

The start, at 2:00 P.M. Friday, was made after a busy morning of work cleaning up last-minute details. The wind was out of the southwest packing a good punch. Most of the boats delayed setting headsails until the last minute. Some hurriedly tucked reefs in their mains, although most of the fleet started under full sail. Even though we had the #2 genoa up, we considered that we were under full sail. The #2 was the real working sail, while the #1 was for light winds up to 10 knots.

CH 1 was 60 miles dead to windward. Shortly after the start we took a short tack into the Bay which paid off handsomely. Then a light spot headed us, putting us right back amongst the leaders. During the afternoon, the wind increased steadily. We began reducing sail. Following one of the sail changes, the odor from the butane stove became prevalent in the galley. A quick inspection showed the valves all "off," with everything apparently in order. It obviously wasn't, though, so without further delay the whole stove went on deck to join the feet, winch handles, and sheet ends in the bottom of the cockpit.

As light faded, *Diana* was well ahead and to leeward, *Hestia* ahead and to windward. We continued to shorten sail throughout the night, as the wind increased to force 8, and more in the gusts. The seas were by turns majestic, vindictive, and greatly confused. We shortened down to working jib and main reefed to the second batten, the smallest it had ever been. In the midst of all this cold wet fury, the English member of our four-man crew said to Dick, "I want you to know, *Rabbit* is the most comfortable boat I have ever been on." At the time it was a preposterous statement—we were anything but comfortable in those Channel seas, slogging against wind, tide, and sea. This was not the weather we were hoping for with the big mainsail. *Rabbit* isn't the type of boat to be driven to windward, as are the deeper and heavier *Diana, Hestia,* and *Cohoe III.*

We were pessimistic about our position with the fleet as daylight arrived Saturday. *Diana* wasn't in sight. There wasn't even a question as to whether she could be behind us. *Hestia* was in sight, but well ahead and to windward. Our morale picked up considerably

To be able to keep the van Beuningens in sight through a night such as that one was certainly encouraging.

The wind slackened with daylight, providing further exercise in adding sail, changing back to the #1 genoa, and unreefing the mainsail. This of course was done in stages, allowing for all the more exercise. We rounded CH 1 at 9:30 A.M. with *Aladdin, Hestia,* and *Alcatraz* ahead of us by 8, 7, and 1 minutes respectively. *Diana* led the fleet, followed 9 minutes later by *Cohoe III,* 23 minutes after that by *Giraglia,* and 8 minutes later by *Ilex II.*

We settled down for the cross Channel spinnaker run to the Nab Tower. We worked constantly to catch the boats ahead, particularly *Alcatraz, Hestia,* and *Aladdin.* With the stove dried out and back in working order, a hot meal was served immediately. Of course, there was the usual lunchtime flap. The spinnaker halyard snap shackle broke, letting the top of the spinnaker fly off to leeward. With some quick action the spinnaker was hauled back on board without getting into the water, and rehoisted on the genoa halyard. The amazing thing was that no one's lunch was even spilled.

That left us with no spinnaker halyard. A discussion followed, through the remainder of lunch, on whether we should attempt to fix it or not. The question was whether the time lost in retrieving and repairing the halyard would be made up. The skipper, as he surveyed the size of those on board, wasn't sure we should waste the time. He was by far the lightest and would surely be "elected" to go aloft. But the conditions were good for such an undertaking now, and one never knew what they would be later. Finally he agreed to go aloft on the main halyard, the only usable halyard to the mast head other than the genoa halyard, which was currently being used for the spinnaker. During his brief stay aloft, Dick looked for wear and tear (none was visible) and investigated the fleet ahead and behind. He claimed to have enjoyed the trip, once again back on the solid deck.

Over this 80-mile leg to the Nab Tower *Diana* gained 13 minutes on *Cohoe III. Giraglia* just failed to get an overlap on *Cohoe III* as they rounded, leaving *Ilex* 25 minutes astern. We rounded the Nab as the sun dropped over the horizon, with *Aladdin, Hestia,* and *Alcatraz* just ahead of us. Actually we were closer to them, but the time difference was exactly the same as when we rounded CH 1.

These slender gains and losses brought a new dimension of excitement and tension to offshore racing. Offshore races have often been won or lost by a margin of only seconds. This closeness only becomes known after the fact, when the handicaps have been applied, but during the race there is hardly any excitement from racing neck and neck with other boats. The One Ton concept brought the constant keenness of one-design racing into offshore racing.

During the evening the sou'wester gradually increased in strength, making for a fast reach back to Le Havre. We hung onto the #1 genoa and full main, trying to catch the three boats just ahead of us. As the seas began to build they were scooped up by the extra large foot in the genoa, but still we pressed on with it. With morning the wind was once again 15 to 20 knots and was a bit more to the west than the southwest. This suggested spinnakers. *Aladdin* and *Alcatraz* had theirs up and found that they had to fall off to leeward in order to carry them. We set the storm spinnaker, a much flatter and somewhat smaller spinnaker than the big one. As it filled it ripped badly, so down it came. We continued on, as did most of the others, under genoa, holding high on our course. The hope was to create a bigger angle from the wind to enable us to carry our spinnaker. *Aladdin* returned to her genoa and hardened up, while *Alcatraz* continued falling off with her spinnaker. *Aladdin*'s and our course were converging, and within an hour we were within a quarter mile of her. She was to leeward and just ahead. Finally *Hestia,* further ahead, decided it was time for her spinnaker. She seemed to carry it all right, and remained on course. We weren't altogether anxious to put up our big spinnaker, especially after the experience we had had broaching with it up at the beginning of the Cowes-Dinard Race. The wind angle was about the same as it had been then, but the wind was now stronger and the seas much larger than they had been in the shelter of the Isle of Wight. *Aladdin* wasn't in any hurry to reset her spinnaker either, probably desiring to get farther to windward before doing so.

With neither of us wanting to be caught unprepared by the other, spinnaker gear appeared and was readied on both boats. Seeing the other follow suit led to the setting of both spinnakers. I suspect that once the spinnaker started out of the bag on *Aladdin* things became active. I know for a fact they did on *Rabbit*. We finally got everything squared away as much as possible and settled down for a hair-raising reach.

Dick, on the tiller, was sensitive to the boat's every move. The trim tab was adjusted to provide some directional help. Someone was on the main sheet and another person on the spinnaker sheet to provide relief on the helm should Dick need it. The timing and feel had to be accurate to a very fine degree to keep the speed, but not to hang on too long and end up broaching. The broach isn't dangerous, but it effectively slows the boat's speed and that was very critical now.

Both boats were really flying, right on the edge of control. Suddenly a wave must have caught *Aladdin* by surprise, for she broached, going over onto her ear and rounding up, losing the wind in her spinnaker, and slowing rapidly. With her spinnaker shaking violently, the spinnaker sheet either broke or came unshackled. As we surged past, barely twenty yards away and just under control ourselves, we held our breath for fear of the same mishap. Remembering our similar situation during the Cowes-Dinard Race, we had mixed emotions: delight that their trouble enabled us to go past, and commiseration with them for having had it happen in such a way.

They retrieved their spinnaker in no time and were right behind us. As we all progressed into the Bay of the Seine the wind came further aft, allowing us to ease off slightly on the sheets. This reduced the likelihood of broaching, but the ride remained very thrilling.

We finished sixth, just ahead of *Aladdin* and *Alcatraz,* with *Hestia* just a few minutes ahead of us. *Diana* won the race, which earned her double points for the ocean race and an additional point for winning.

She was now leading with 37 points. *Hestia* and *Giraglia* were tied for second with 35 points each.

The third race, another 30-miler, was an Olympic-type triangle, twice around. The wind was 15 to 20 knots from the southwest at the start and held throughout the race. We were too anxious and were over early. The fight was between *Hestia* and *Diana* right from the beginning. *Giraglia* wasn't quite up to the heavier Sparkman and Stephens boats in wind of this strength and seas of this size. *Diana* made the best start and led all around the course. *Hestia* hung onto her stern, but could never pass. The rest of the fleet strung out behind.

The One Ton Cup went to *Diana* and would be held in Copenhagen, Denmark, next summer. It would be an exciting year in Copenhagen: the One Ton Cup, the finish of the Transatlantic and Tall Ships races, the 5.5 championships, and the 100th year of the Royal Danish Yacht Club. The final standings were *Diana* 52, *Hestia* 48¼, *Giraglia* 46, *Alcatraz* 43¼, *Cohoe III* 42¼, *Ilex II* 37.

The following afternoon, Wednesday, we set sail for Cowes. The Channel Race's start was Friday afternoon off Portsmouth, and we had to change mainsails and boom and obtain necessary stores. There was never any time for relaxing, but with four of us on board for the trip back Dick and I were looking forward to 2 hours on and 6 off—a welcome change from our previous passage into Cowes.

Rabbit, *with R.O.R.C. main. Note genoa hanked on inside the bow pulpit.*

5. Cowes Week

WITH the wind still blowing 15 to 20 knots from the southwest we departed for Cowes. It was an easy reach across the Channel, but it wasn't restful. We had plenty of time to spend in our bunks, but little sleep. During the evening the wind came on much stronger and the seas built up short and steep. By midnight we had rolled the main down to the second batten and removed all headsails. *Rabbit* was at ease with the conditions, there was no fuss or struggle, and the deck remained relatively dry. We must have been making good speed, for we made the crossing in excellent time.

On entering the Solent we decided on powering to Cowes, dead to windward and against the tide. This didn't prove very successful, for we ran out of gasoline soon after the sails were furled and stowed. Resetting the sails, we beat along the Isle of Wight coast and into Cowes, where we tied up in the trots. This is no easy task under the best of conditions—that is, under power and with no wind or current. As we were under sail with both ample wind and current at right angles to each other, we had an interesting time of it. We were anxious to get as near to Larlow's Yard as possible and on the inside of the trots as well. Luckily the trots were not crowded, nor was there much activity as we entered; thus we had ample space to maneuver in for the single pass at the place we had selected to tie up. We picked the biggest boat we could find and secured alongside with little trouble or scraping of topsides. Then we obtained supplies and fuel, and reverted to our regular mainsail and boom.

Later that afternoon, we departed for Portsmouth for the start of the Channel Race. The engine did not run smoothly as it started, but we decided that there was only some air or dirt in the lines which would clear up right away. Instead, the engine stopped altogether as we cleared the trots and immediately had one of the island ferries bearing down on us. Whatever the sequence of his whistles meant, no one on board *Rabbit* knew. It was obvious, though, that he would not, and could not, keep clear of us. Sail was set in record time.

On entering Portsmouth we tried the engine again. By experimenting we found that it would just keep running if the throttle and choke remained wide open. We coughed and sputtered our way into the fleet moored off the Camper and Nicholson Yard, expecting the engine to stop at any moment. A closer inspection revealed that the fuel tank had been filled with gas oil (diesel fuel) instead of gasoline (petrol). The problem was going to have to wait until after the Channel Race.

On our way out of Portsmouth Harbor, as we headed for the starting line, a rope fouled the rudder, jamming it hard to port. If it wasn't one thing it was another. With the rudder hard over we began circling in the very narrow entrance. Portsmouth is always busy with ferries and ships trying to keep to their schedules, hurrying in both directions. It was unusually busy at that moment with the racing fleet pouring out to the starting area. With the armada bearing down on us, whistles blasting, John Everett was overboard in an instant to clear away the mess.

Our class started last, at slack water and with very little wind. The Class I boats were only a mile or so ahead of us, for they had had the last of the incoming tide to fight in the light northerly. As we glided past the forts, a fresh breeze soon had the whole fleet under spinnakers reaching for the Owers Light Ship. The sunset was beautiful, with the many-colored spinnakers standing out brightly. We rounded the Owers in good standing and followed the larger boats east along the coast, hard on the wind. The next mark was the Royal Sovereign Light Ship off my friend Beachy Head.

Some boats tacked inshore, although most of the fleet stood out on the port tack, the tack closest to the rhumb line. We were carrying the #1 genoa, which at times was more sail than we wanted. *Rabbit* was designed to get the greatest speed when sailed upright, with the lee rail 6 to 8 inches above the water rather than under it. When designing the headsails a miscalculation had been made in determining the step down from the #1 genoa to the #2 genoa. The gap between the two sails was too large, leaving us either overpowered or underpowered in certain conditions. This leg was one of those times. We were also still learning how to sail *Rabbit*.

Channel Race

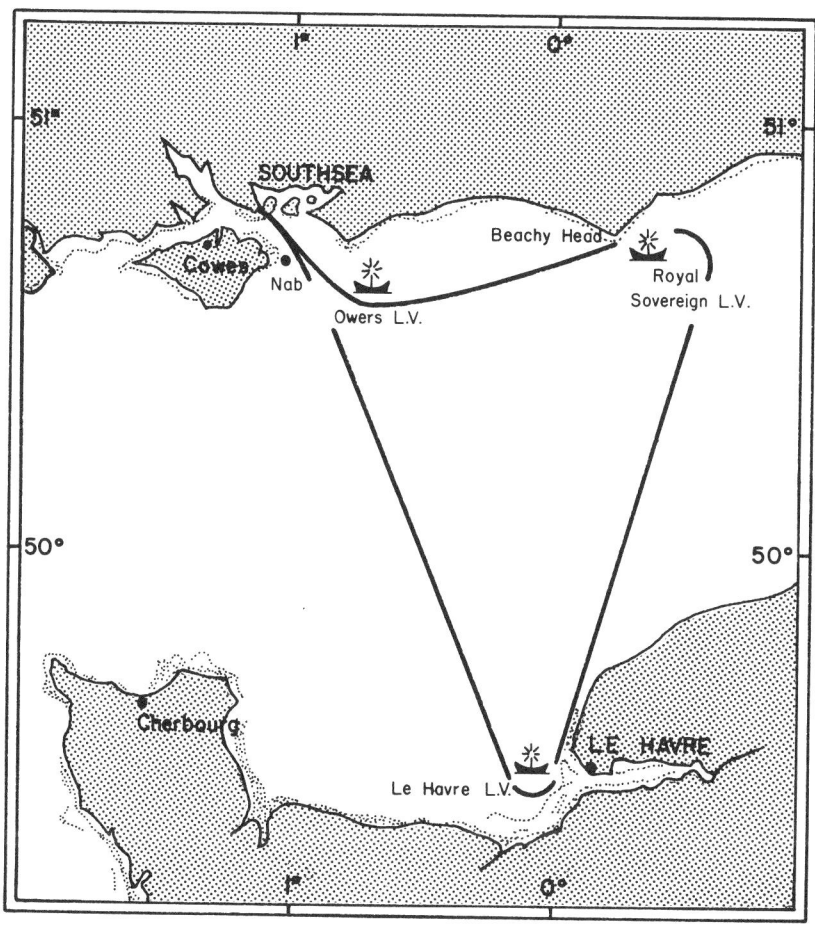

The array of running lights didn't improve our spirits as they pulled ahead. We had forgotten, though, that most of them were larger boats and should go faster. Fortunately we had no troubles with Beachy Head, and rounded the Royal Sovereign Light Vessel just after dawn with a fading breeze. Ahead of us was a long string of boats under spinnaker. There was also a long line behind us, but that was where they should all be.

All day we ghosted along under spinnaker with 5 to 8 knots of wind. These were the conditions that *Rabbit* was designed to excel in. We passed quite a number of boats during this run to the Le Havre Light Ship. (The race is made much more interesting than the course instructions indicate. The light ship is removed during the summer months and is replaced with a buoy. The buoy gives off a radio beacon, but the light itself is very small. Locating this mark in the middle of the Bay of the Seine can be a very difficult task.) We rounded in excellent position.

The weather forecasts were predicting that the wind would shift out of the north into the west and southwest during the night. We could have just fetched the course back across the Channel to the Nab Tower, but, gambling that the weather forecasts were going to be accurate, we held below the course with sheets slightly eased. This was our chance to show *Rabbit*'s real boat speed.

Speed we got, but the wind did not swing to the southwest in time. Landfall found us several miles to the east of the Owers Light Ship. With the tide about to turn against us we kept on toward the shallows inside the Owers. With our detailed chart of the area, good lighting, and a constant watch on both the water and the fathometer we sailed in amongst the shallows. Another boat a slight distance offshore and to windward of us tacked away. She quickly disappeared out into the Channel with the tide.

Without mishap we hugged the beach all the way around to Portsmouth, finishing shortly after noon. Although we ended up 30th at the finish, the race highlighted *Rabbit*'s two principal design theories: to excel in light air and pure boat speed over speed-made-good to windward. In a 116-boat fleet we were first on corrected time at the

The trots at Cowes 51 weeks of the year
The trots during Cowes Week (Below)

first mark, then plummeted to 52nd place on the windward leg to the Royal Sovereign and then climbed all the way back to third on the cross Channel spinnaker run. The big disappointment was to learn from boats that had stood high early on the leg back to the Nab that their wind did swing into the southwest late that evening, as had been predicted.

Sailing into Cowes this time, we found the trots filled with boats of all sizes and shapes. We wanted an inside berth and somehow managed one. Activity was unbelievable; the famous Cowes Week had started.

The week provides something for everyone afloat and ashore. For nine days, the otherwise quiet little town of Cowes becomes a beehive of activity, overwhelmed with crowds both afloat and ashore. It is undoubtedly the most exciting week of racing anywhere. Each year records are broken for the number of starters, visiting foreign yachts, and the associated color and atmosphere. Spectators crowd into the town to take in the busy scene. They stay to watch from early morning the starts and finishes, and to wander among the shops and pubs. Everyone watches the big boats, but the week would be nothing without the supporting cast of small cruisers, the Solent Sunbeams, the Swallows, the Victories, the X boats, Dragons, and cats. They all race seriously for important cups and are the mainstay of Cowes Week.

Monday, we decided, would be a day of rest. It was, too, for it rained all day, making life cramped on board with little other than shopping to do ashore. The close damp confines of below decks were made even less bearable by the addition of the smell of gas oil when we drained the contents of the fuel tank. In refilling the tank we used the highest octane gasoline we could find. Still it wouldn't start.

Tuesday, with five males and the three Carter women aboard, we went out for a Cowes day race. The course was a triangle, twice around, starting into the southwest wind and against the tide. The question was which coast to hug on the beat to the first mark. Chippy Davie, who knew the area, recommended the mainland shore. Despite this, we had a poor start, late for the line and too near the Island shore.

We settled down under the #1 genoa, hanked on outside the lifelines, and headed across to the other shore. *Rabbit* was moving well, outfooting and pointing as high as those around us. We were pleasantly surprised that she was competitive in this type of racing. As we converged on the shore we discovered, much to our excitement, that we were leading Class III boat for boat and were up amongst Class II. There was no time for relaxing, for *Hestia, Yeoman XIII,* and *Sunmaid IV* were right on our heels. There was a continuous parade of boats fighting their way westward, staying as close to shore as they dared. With such a mass of boats, a conglomeration from all three classes, there was a continuous chorus of "Starboard," "Water room," and "Right of way." To add to the confusion, some of the boats eased to a stop on the soft Solent mud.

In the thick of Class II we had a boat-for-boat battle with *Hestia* and *Yeoman XIII* for the lead in our class. We were so close that our positions changed with every tack. At one point we found ourselves just off *Yeoman XIII*'s windward quarter and headed for the shore. It was nip and tuck whether we would drop back into her backwind or slide up and bother her wind. For several minutes our positions hung in balance. Then we began to move up. Just as the balance was broken, Robin Asher, who was sailing *Yeoman XIII,* called for water room. One cannot argue with this request, so we tacked, although we questioned that it was needed quite so soon. *Yeoman XIII* held on for a couple of boat lengths prior to tacking herself, leaving her clear of our backwind. Dick immediately realized that he had made a bad move; he should have acknowledged Owen's request with a comment to the effect that he could tack anytime he needed and we would keep clear. By doing it this way, as *Yeoman XIII* tacked we would also tack, with her ending up in our backwind on our windward quarter—assuming that each boat tacked flawlessly.

In our case tacking was made even more difficult by the method we used, as the #1 genoa was attached outside the lifelines. This certainly added pressure to the already tense and exciting beat.

Our tacking procedure went something like this. For each tack my station was by the mast. With Dick's "Ready about," I would allow 6 inches of slack in the genoa halyard between the halyard cleat and the winch. The winch handle was left in the winch for instant use, but had to be left in such a position as to avoid snagging the flapping genoa sheet on the tack. When Dick started the "Hard-a-lee," I would release the slack 6 inches in the halyard. This slackened the genoa luff just enough to allow the tack to slide off the rabbit ear. I would rush to the bow, unhook the tack from one ear, lift it up and over the pulpit, and down to the new leeward rabbit ear. This was done with the foredeck at all angles, the genoa crossing over my back, and the tack flapping about in my hands. Then I had to get back to the mast and crank up those 6 inches on the halyard before the genoa filled on the new tack.

I considered conspiring with the boys on the genoa sheet to slow down, but the excitement was contagious. We were making so many short tacks that many times I didn't have time to recleat the halyard after each tack. "Playing the sheets" is common enough, but this way of "playing the halyard" was quite new to me.

The procedure worked far better than we had expected. It delighted us to be able to sustain a tacking duel with *Hestia* and *Yeoman XIII*. My shins, toes, knees, and knuckles showed considerable wear and tear as we rounded the windward mark, but I didn't mind.

Our course and that of *Drumbeat* (Class I) converged on one of our offshore starboard tacks. Jack Knights, who had raced with us in Le Havre, was on *Drumbeat*'s bow, peering out from under her genoa. Although she could easily have cleared our bow, she chose to cover us by tacking directly in front of us. Maybe she was getting even, for a couple of tacks earlier we had forced her to tack on a port and starboard encounter. There was little we could do. We certainly didn't want to stay behind her and there was no possible way to pass; she carried three times as much sail as we did. We tacked. Upon getting clear of *Drumbeat* our attention returned to our own class. There were *Hestia* and *Sunmaid IV* standing out into the Channel toward a buoy. Ours!

We rounded third, 2 minutes behind *Sunmaid IV* and *Hestia*.

Yeoman XIII was right behind us. We held on to them during the next 4 legs. In spite of all our efforts we couldn't catch up, nor did the boats behind us gain. The wind had increased slightly, making the #1 genoa just too much sail and the #2 genoa not quite enough. During the last reach and beat to the finish we slowly lost our grip and dropped back. After all the calculations were made we finished fifth, behind *Sunmaid IV, Hestia, Yeoman XIII* and *Meon Maid II.*

We were disappointed to have dropped back on the last legs, but were excited that *Rabbit* was competitive in concentrated around-the-buoy racing. We were all keyed up for Wednesday's race: the Royal Yacht Squadron's 150th Anniversary Race.

At the start it was critical to hug the Isle of Wight shore, out of the adverse current. As the inshore end of the line (about 20 yards off the beach) was the most advantageous place to start, the confusion created there was tremendous. We found a hole and sneaked through as the gun was fired. This gave us a jump out with the leaders and away from the mass of boats all trying to stay as close to shore as possible. Through recklessness, courage, stupidity, or just fear of being overrun by the mass of hulls and canvas, we stayed closer to the beach than the rest. This paid off, for we worked our way into third, just behind *Hestia* and *Sunmaid IV*. During the following legs we could not catch these well-sailed boats. This time we didn't slide back during the last leg and finished third boat-for-boat in our class and right beside *Tonnere de Breskens,* who was second in Class II.

Hestia remained by the line upon finishing in order to take the elapsed time between our finishes. We hoped we had beaten them on corrected time. They were inclined to agree when we met them on shore on the way to sign our race declarations.

Upon getting to the Race Headquarters I discovered that we were not listed as having finished, even though boats which had finished ahead of and behind us were.

I tried to think what we could have done wrong. We had been on *Hestia*'s and *Sunmaid IV*'s heels all day. I was beginning to think of the results of the North Sea Race. My thoughts weren't happy.

To my surprise and relief it was suggested that we go up to the Royal Yacht Squadron and talk with the timekeepers. Up on the terrace in front of the club, overlooking the finish line, we discussed my plight. In less than ten minutes we pieced together the story. All mystery and antagonistic feelings completely vanished. As we had crossed the line, another boat in a smaller class crossed also. She received the gun due her for being first in her class. The man on the line called out our number and time, along with those for the other boats finishing. Each class has a separate person keeping track of that class's finishing times. The timekeeper for Class III wasn't sure of our exact time, so he asked for the seconds again on sail 2198 (*Rabbit*'s number). He was given a time and a correction to the number by the man on the line, who happened to be looking at the boat that finished right behind us, sail number 2188, 10 digits lower than *Rabbit*'s. The timekeeper's erasure on the time sheet was very evident and a mistake that was understandably easy to make. Without any to-do the Committee re-entered us as finishing and used *Tonnere de Breskens*' finishing time as ours.

I returned with the man from Race Headquarters, who fed our time into "the machine," a computer located in London. The results: *Rabbit* first, *Hestia* second, *Sunmaid IV* third.

Thursday we were out again. It was an anticlimactic day after Wednesday's win. We finished sixth, behind *Hestia* who won and *Sunmaid IV* who finished fifth. The day was made when, sailing into the trots, I happened to try starting the engine once again. It worked! We tied up in the trots in a normal fashion, under power, and had even more trouble than when we had sailed in.

6. Fastnet

FASTNET Rock is a goal for ocean racers and a landmark for all sailing within sight of Ireland's wild and beautiful southwestern coast. The light stands some 175 feet above the sea almost 5 miles out from Cape Clear, the southwesterly point of Ireland. The formidable shape of the Fastnet, a stack of rock rising 91 feet above sea level, is surrounded by numerous reefs and subterranean ridges which cause strong currents and a lot of surf, even on calm days. Cape Clear possessed a light long before Fastnet Rock, but because of its placement on top of the Cape's high headland it was obscured by continual low clouds and mist. Due to the strategic position held by this corner of Ireland's coast in relation to transatlantic shipping, it was decided to build a light on the off-lying rock.

George Halpin, an engineer to the Port of Dublin, started work on the construction of a cast-iron cylindrical building in 1848. Because of the many formidable difficulties involved in this task, the lighthouse was not completed until January 1854. Halpin's structure was built on the very top of the Rock and housed a revolving light of 38,000 candlepower.

On numerous occasions during its first years of service the lighthouse gave cause for alarm as to its safety. Incidents were reported when it "trembled like a leaf" on being hit by huge waves. Once a cup full of coffee sailed off the table during a storm; another time a rough sea broke away a 3-ton piece of rock which was then lifted by a wave and smashed against the tower.

Improvements were made to strengthen the tower, and it survived gale after gale. By 1891 many of the cast iron plates were very loose and many of the bolts had sheared off. The Fastnet's lighthouse was near collapse.

William Douglas, then engineer in charge of lighthouses, designed a new one of stone, to be built on the hardest part of the Rock, a ledge 6 inches below the highwater mark. In 1896 the first party of workers landed on the Rock. The granite from which the new tower was built was quarried in Cornwall and cut to size. Each block weighed between 4 and 5 tons. These were dovetailed and set

Fastnet Rock

up to ensure a proper fit. The blocks were then marked and sent to the Rock. Transferring these large stones from the tender to the Rock presented a problem, overcome by crating each one in turn to avoid damage to it. These crates were then dropped into the sea close alongside the Fastnet, attached by a rope to the crane on the Rock, and hauled to the surface right at the lighthouse's foundation. Some 2,044 blocks were transferred in this manner, a total weight of 4,633 tons.

Finally a Chance Brothers lantern of 750,000 candlepower was installed. During the years since, the light has been increased in power to 1,300,000 candlepower and has a visibility of 18 nautical miles in clear conditions. In mist and bad visibility an explosive fog signal sounds every 3 minutes in warning of its dangers.

The first race around Fastnet Rock was in 1925. It was organized by Weston Martyr and George Martin, owner of *Jolie Brise,* eventually a three-time winner. Seven boats started from Ryde in that first race. They were all gaff-rigged with deep draft, so aptly described by Alfred Loomis as the "sort that British cruising men love, able to put to sea and stay there, but designed with no particular emphasis on speed." Following that eventful race, at a dinner at the Royal Western Yacht Club, the formation of the Ocean Racing Club was announced. The first race was so successful that plans were immediately made for another in 1926. In that year the entrance of *Primrose IV,* an Alden schooner from Boston, started the race on the international trend that has continued to the present. In 1965 the fleet had grown to 151 starters from 13 countries.

We started Saturday evening with a moderate southerly breeze and with the tide soon to turn favorable. Once again the ploy at the start was to be in as close to the Isle of Wight shore as possible. We got clear at the start, and after several short tacks close to the spectator-covered beach we were leading our class. As we cleared Egypt Point the wind swung to the south and south-southeast, which was just our cup of tea. With the #1 genoa eased slightly we romped down the Solent amongst Class II.

On clearing the Solent we headed for Portland Bill, hoping to

Class III Fastnet Race start. Rabbit *is the only boat showing any lively movement.*

clear it before 0145 when the tide would begin to run foul. Just as the sun dropped below the horizon, *Camille,* an Australian Admiral's Cup team member and scratch boat in Class III, came barrelling past. To add insult to injury, she poured past to leeward of us without breaking her stride.

All Sunday the wind was light and variable with numerous holes. Throughout the day we had Class I and II boats in sight. There were no Class III boats to be seen. Where had *Camille* gone? The trip along the coast consisted of making tides around critical points and of keeping moving. In the holes, most of the boats around us stalled out. With our big half-ounce spinnaker we didn't stop until we finally became completely becalmed off Plymouth.

When the wind returned, it came in, surprisingly, from the southeast. This whittled down our lead in Class III, but our morale soared as dawn broke on the waters off the Lizard. We were still among the hot boats in Classes I and II. The wind held in the southeast and increased in strength as we cleared Land's End at 0700 and headed for

Fastnet Race

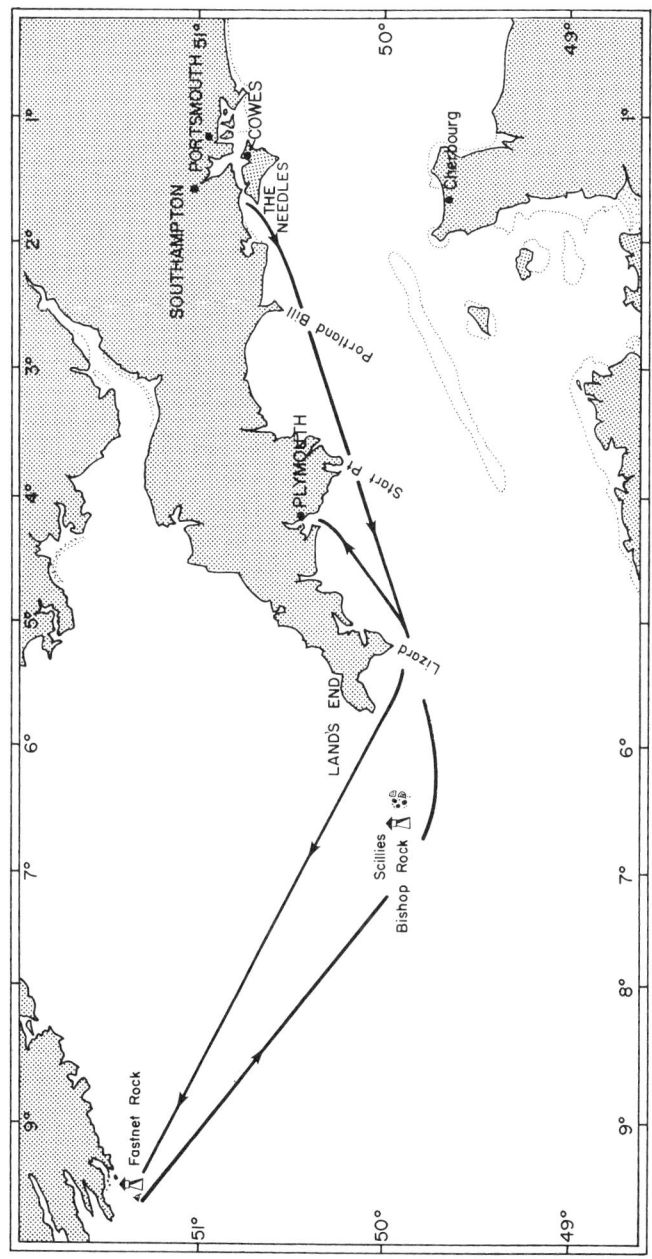

Fastnet Rock. By noon the southeast seas had built up and were angling in just aft of our quarter while the southwesterly swells that were still running were approaching forward of the beam. Every so often they would get in phase. Steering became difficult, but with the spade rudder *Rabbit* responded very well, although the helmsman's right arm and shoulder received quite a workout. This was the first time we had sailed *Rabbit* downwind in a seaway—a test to which *Rabbit* responded easily.

The helmsman's objective was to maintain course with the maximum speed without broaching. It was a temptation to bear off several degrees to get a better lift from the seas for possible surfing. To compensate for any weak moments was difficult, since our course was already as high as we could comfortably carry the spinnaker. We did have several great rides, during which green water surged up to the height of the boom on either side, just aft of the mast. The speed indicator was pegged at 10 knots much of the time.

Shortly before the change of the watch at 8:00 P.M. the spinnaker halyard parted. Quick work retrieved the spinnaker before it could fall into the water. This problem had been anticipated and a hole had been drilled in the masthead fitting for a shackle and halyard block. Once again Dick was hoisted aloft. On top of the wildly arching spar, he screwed the new shackle to the masthead and rove a spare spinnaker halyard. This one was completely external. Somehow he accomplished the task in quick order without dropping the shackle, pin, or block and without losing his own hold on the spar. On returning to deck all he would say about his recent trip was how marvellous it was to watch *Rabbit* from aloft. Had we nothing better to do I might have hoisted him back up there until he tired of the sight, but we had the spinnaker to reset.

An hour and a half later, with the spinnaker breaking frequently, the guy snap shackle broke. As we lowered the spinnaker again the sail's tack fitting ripped several large holes in the spinnaker. The genoa was set as the spinnaker disappeared below. This change of headsails required that we head up 10 degrees in an attempt to maintain our speed. Needle, thread, and Rip Stop became the focus of attention for the next several hours.

With morning the wind moderated quickly and we hoisted the light weather spinnaker, the only whole one we had left. For a while we held our breath, hoping that the half-ounce material would hold. It did, and soon the wind dropped to a strength perfect for the light sail.

I spotted the Rock, sticking through a hole in the haze that covered the Irish coast, shortly before noon. We squared away for it and rounded in good company: *Whistler of Pagent,* scratch boat in Class II, *Tonnere de Breskens,* and other Class I and II boats. We still hadn't seen *Camille.* Was she miles ahead of us?

The forecast was for winds to increase to force 4 and 5 pulling into the south and southwest. The present southerly wasn't altogether to our liking, for it made a beat to Bishop Rock, 150 miles away. After rounding the Rock we took a hitch to the south, well away from the direct course to Bishop Rock that almost everyone was following on the other tack. Just after we changed to our #2 genoa the dark gray clouds rolled away and the wind lifted us. But, more significantly, the wind moderated. We shifted back to the big 180% genoa and sailed, close hauled all night, as fast as or faster than every boat in sight.

As we approached the Scilly Islands we were headed and found ourselves in the dismal position of beating straight into a foul current. It took us 9 hours to round Bishop Rock. Part of our delay was staying outside the rocks that make up the Scillies. We were unsure which rocks were included in the Scillies according to the rules. Later we saw several boats dodge inside them; apparently they do so even when fog covers the current-swept area.

Once again *Camille* steamed past us as we fought against the tide to round Bishop Rock. It was a welcome relief to get around and slacken sheets for the reach to Plymouth. But it wasn't to be that easy. We were headed twice and ended up beating nearly the whole way.

At 1333 we crossed the line, thankful to be in. Later, when tied up

The winning crew: (left to right) John Carter, Peter Moore, Dick Carter, Terry Brownrigg, John Everett, Sandy Weld (seated)

in the Basin relaxing, we estimated that we had won our class and come in second overall, right behind *Quiver IV*. Too bad not to have beaten *Quiver IV*, but if you don't tie a race together the chances of winning are slim. We felt we were still tuning *Rabbit*, getting to know her likes and dislikes. None of our previous races had been particularly well tied together, and we counted 15 hours that we had "given" away during this race one way or another.

It wasn't until several hours later that we learned we had won after all. We couldn't believe it. The Fastnet Race is such an important event, and to win it seemed impossible.

The local press claimed that the race had been an upside-down drifting match. The typical race (if there is such a thing) is a tough beat out to the Rock and a sleigh-ride home. They dubbed it upside-down in deference to the Australians, and a drifting match because such a small boat won the race. There was ample light air, but major damage was also caused to some boats.

A spinnaker guy had parted on *Outlaw* during the blow running to the Rock. When the pole slammed into the forestay it bent 45 degrees. The helmsman was unable to control her in the sudden lurch that followed, and the resulting flying gybe brought her boom up against the after shroud. The double jerk and terrific compression snapped the mast 10 feet above the deck.

Seeing *Outlaw* in trouble, *Vagabonde* squared away and ran dead before the wind to give whatever aid was needed. She also gybed unexpectedly and snapped her boom in two in the water. With *Vagabonde* heeled over due to the all standing gybe, the spinnaker took charge and ripped the pole from the mast, sending it through the mainsail. At least three of the five boats that did not finish were in Class I. *Gitana IV* also had her troubles with weather. First her spinnaker pole broke the forestay, and then the spinnaker halyard swivel went. She not only didn't retire from the race, but she set a new elapsed course record of 3 days, 9 hours, and 40 minutes.

Here are a few interesting statistics about the event. It was the largest fleet ever to compete in that race: 151 starters with 149 finishers. *Rabbit* was the ninth smallest boat in the entire fleet, beating on a boat-for-boat basis 4 yachts in Class I, 26 in Class II, and all but one of the 69 in Class III. On corrected time we were first around the Fastnet Rock and, despite the preponderance of windward work over the last 250 miles to the finish, we lengthened our lead by half an hour.

It was a wonderful way to end a great season. Dick was off to the United States and I was off, riding on cloud nine. Before leaving Plymouth I jumped at the chance to sign on with Geof Pattinson, who was shipping *Fanfare* from England to Australia for the Sydney-Hobart.

Greek Islands

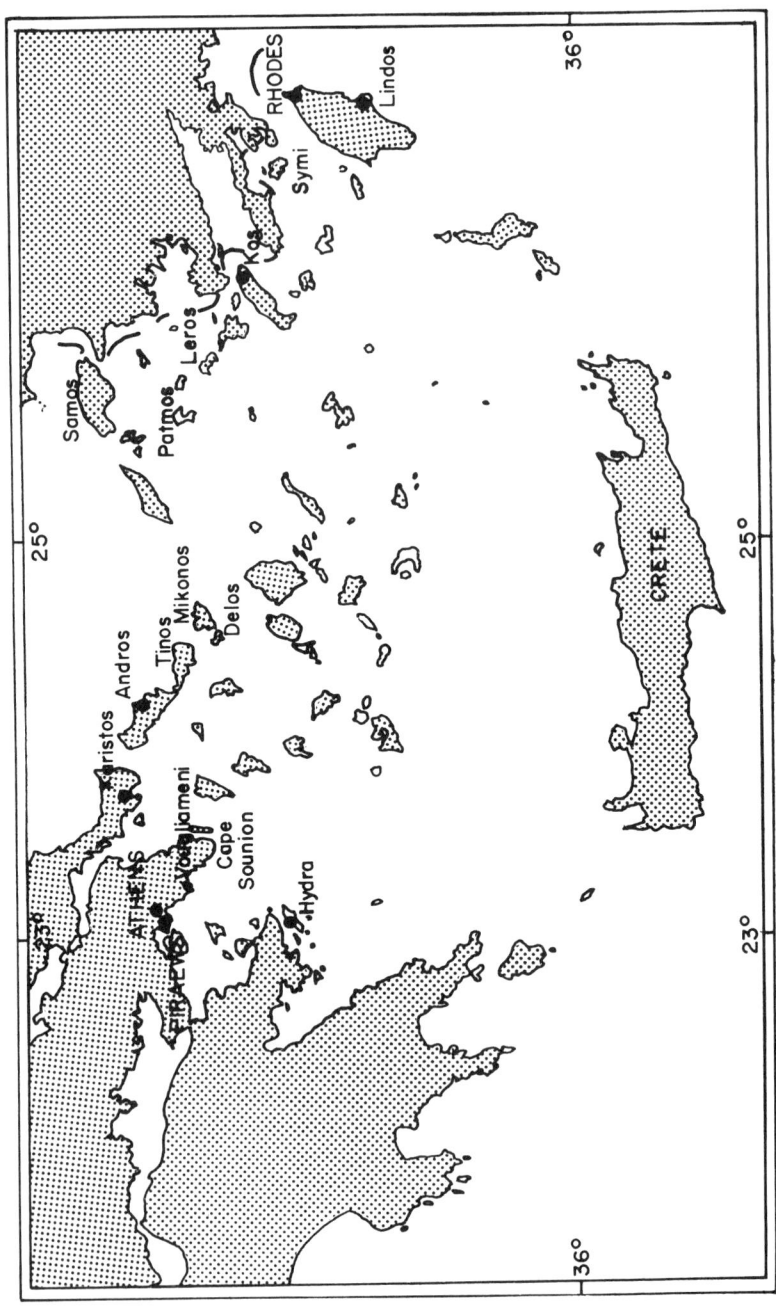

7. Gearing Down

I wasn't allowed to rest on cloud nine for long. The next Sunday I was off on *Caper* for the Plymouth-La Rochelle Race. *Caper* was by far the largest boat I'd ever been on. I was quickly called to task as we practiced gybing the spinnaker in the near non-existent northerly prior to the race's start. About to haul the spinnaker sheet in by hand to attach it to the pole as it swung across, I very soon learned that gear on larger boats gets bigger fast and that the stresses and strains build up even faster.

Caper, owned by New York businessman Irving Pratt, had sailed across the Atlantic in early summer to be a member of the American Admiral's Cup team. She had been raced hard, with the renowned 12-meter helmsman, Bus Mosbacher, putting her through her paces. The La Rochelle Race was a gearing down for her as well as for me. The big effort was over.

The weather was obliging, for we set the spinnaker at the start and didn't take it down until we crossed the finish line. We stayed in La Rochelle for several days "resting." The passage on to Lisbon was even more enjoyable as we moved further south. We had almost all types of weather to begin with, from flat calm to force 8, during which we hove to for 24 hours. After rounding Cape Finisterre it was a downhill ride all the way to Lisbon. Depending on the strength of the wind, we maintained 10 knots under a combination of sails ranging from staysail and trysail to full main and spinnaker.

The sky was bright blue and the temperature was warm. During the whole time I was offshore on *Rabbit* I had never been out of long pants, usually with winter underwear and several sweaters. But this trip on *Caper* was quite different. There were the usual crises, but they were soon forgotten in the relaxed atmosphere and warm sun. We sailed into Lisbon Wednesday morning and were welcomed warmly by the Nautical Yacht Club.

From Portugal I flew to Rhodes, where I had arranged to join the crew of *Velila.* The first day on Rhodes I hired a motor bike and followed the east coast to Lindos, a small town on the southeast coast of Rhodes. On one side of the town is a lovely crescent beach where

I swam and had lunch. On the other side is its acropolis, which climbs right out of the town to the top of a high headland looking out over the beautiful blue-green Mediterranean. The acropolis originated with Danaos and his fifty sons and daughters when they fled from Egypt. It contains a history of the islands in epitome, with a beautiful colonnade, the temple of Athena Lindia, a Byzantine church, a Castle of the Knights, and Turkish fortifications.

In the town itself the "streets" are only wide enough for pedestrians or mules. The buildings are all old, some dating back to the seventeenth century. Many of these have courtyards laid out in black and white mosaic patterns.

The following day I investigated the city of Rhodes, the old and the new. The old city is completely within its old walls, which are still intact. Walking through the labyrinth of markets, mosques, and fountains one is made very aware also of the modern Rhodes, adjacent to the old city, with new buildings and construction everywhere and all the hustle-bustle of any tourist city.

Rhodes faces the small port of Mandraki, which was the ancient harbor. The entry is probably best known for the huge statue that once stood there, the Colossus of Rhodes, one of the Seven Wonders of the Ancient World. The harbor is very active with visiting yachts, fishing caiques, and commerce ships, carrying either tourists or merchandise.

As I was enjoying myself at one of the many sidewalk cafés, *Velila* sailed into the harbor. She is a Rhodes-designed 77-foot ketch built of steel in 1949. The large beam and shallow draft (6½ feet with the board up) made her ideal for charter work, which she had been doing in those waters for many years. *Velila*'s permanent crew consisted of Hod Fuller, owner, captain, engineer, and host; Yanny, cook; Filepo, steward and deck hand when needed; and Yogo, deck hand and first-rate seaman. I joined the crew as chief flunky to Yogo.

Velila's accommodations included a master double stateroom, two doubles, and a single stateroom aft. A separate deck house lounge was just forward of the midship cockpit, and a dining saloon was forward of that. Then came the galley and crew quarters. There were three heads, all with showers and hot and cold running water. This was a completely new dimension of sailing for me.

Normally everyone managed two swims a day; I usually took a dip before breakfast as well. The water is beautiful, in color and temperature both. The Aegean has a higher salt content than most other bodies of water. I for one liked this, for I didn't sink as fast, nor does the salt bother me.

The charterees, three couples from Louisville, Kentucky, arrived Tuesday morning for a two-week cruise back to Athens. We shoved off after stowing their belongings and powered the short distance to a cove on Symi, a small island which lies off the Turkish coast. We anchored in the nearly land-locked cove in 35 feet of water. It was amazing to see the anchor lying on the bottom with the chain curving up to the surface and *Velila*'s bow. A monastery on the shore of the cove maintains the "town" for local Greek tourists who cannot afford the bigger vacation areas. Beside the monastery there is a general store, one hotel, and several boarding houses. A few homes are spread out on the hillside behind, with a very attractive swimming beach at one end of the town.

Our next stop was off a point in Turkey near the town of Kumalt, where the Romans used to have a large thriving city. To me there seemed to be nothing left, just rock rubble. To the archaeologist the ruins are very productive and much can be found there pertaining to their history. Diving in the cove was a lad who had been studying in Vienna. He was gathering quite a number of old relics off the bottom. He hadn't solved his problem of getting them home, for both Greece and Turkey have laws forbidding the export or sale of such relics. As we left he was having trouble with the Turkish soldiers who discovered that he was not spear fishing.

We anchored inside the small man-made harbor of Kos, which was built many centuries ago. Upon investigating we found an interesting tourist town, one of relatively modern design due to a devastating earthquake in 1933. Scattered throughout the town are remains of Hellenistic and Byzantine sanctuaries, the Castle of the Knights of Rhodes, and Turkish mosques and fountains. Beside an eighteenth-century mosque, still in good repair, is the strangest sprawled-out tree I have even seen. Its trunk is about 10 feet in diameter and stands no more than 50 feet high. The trunk has been split by the Maltamei winds, the limbs are all split, and each of the split limbs has split several more times. Hippocrates, who was born on the island, is supposed to have sat under this tree in the fifth century B.C.

Velila operated on daylight saving time in order to use as much of the daylight as possible. The daily routine started with a swim, for those who could manage it, before the 8:30 breakfast. We got under way during breakfast or shortly thereafter, depending on how far it was to our midday stop at some interesting island for a swim, lunch, siesta, and a trip ashore. The evening would find us at another island for the night.

My normal routine was to take a swim before breakfast, then wipe the salt off the varnish. On a 77-footer there can be a tremendous amount of bright work, but fortunately *Velila* didn't have much. For the rest of the day I'd help Yogo if he could find anything to do, or I'd find something myself. We didn't do much sailing; only twice did we have the jib and mizzen up during the two weeks. Experience has proven that most charterers aren't very keen on beating or drifting; they like to travel comfortably to see the sights. The wind at this time of year doesn't come up until noon, and when it does it is strong and from the north, the direction in which we were going.

Another of my tasks was to help pull up the anchor. I watched the electric windlass and then hoisted the anchor onto the deck by the davits. Also I washed down the teak decks every three or four days. Once in a while I'd steer, when the automatic pilot wasn't on or when everyone was sleeping after lunch.

For me, sailing had taken on a new slowness but the scenery and surroundings made up for it. The total combination of brown sand and rock islands rising out of the clear brilliant blue sea with a background of sharp blue sky was unbelievable. Adding to the beauty of it all was a haze that surrounded the base of each island, caused by the contrast between the hot sand and rocks which make up most of the islands, and the cooler water.

The most awe-inspiring sight I saw was from atop the mountain on Delos. The full 360-degree panorama includes many small islands and channels in the foreground, behind which are larger bodies of water with bigger islands seeming to rise out of nothing because of the haze around their bases. It is as close to a live fantasy scene as anything I have ever seen.

The island of Delos has the ruins of what was one of the major sea ports a few centuries ago. There is still a recognizable outline of the old city, in which one can distinguish some of the structures, although they have no roofs. One of the old courtyards has a mosaic of the Dolphin of Delos, a dolphin swimming around the stem of an anchor. Excavation is still going on there.

During August and September the prevailing wind blows from the north, turning during September and October into the stronger Maltamei winds. The mornings are usually very still. Around midday the wind comes up very suddenly and with considerable force. The wind whistles around the ends of the islands, producing very shifty conditions. The lee sides of the islands don't produce the expected shelter from the winds unless one goes within about 25 yards of the rocky shore. This skirting of the shore the natives call "coastacoasta." We did it quite frequently. There is hardly any fear of hitting bottom, for the coastlines of the Aegean Islands are very steep. Almost without exception one cannot see bottom 25 yards off the islands, and often the depth sounder cannot find it. Off some of the islands it is difficult and even impossible to find an anchorage; the water is just too deep. Most of the harbors are along the shores of a bay, which has built up to a depth suitable for anchoring.

One of them is the beautiful harbor of Patmos. It is a busy tourist town, mainly because of the eleventh-century monastery atop a mountain overlooking the town and the Church of the Apocalypse which enshrines the cave where St. John received the Revelations. I joined the tourists and climbed to the Church of the Apocalypse; others rode donkeys up.

I then followed the donkeys to the famous monastery, which has not been plundered since the eleventh century. The monastery is intact and very much in use, not just as a tourist attraction. There is a noble eleventh century icon of St. John the Divine. The rich treasury has many fine Byzantine jewels and examples of embroidery. There is also a fine carved screen of the early nineteenth century. The library is famous for the Codex Porphyrius of the Gospel, 33 leaves containing most of St. Mark's gospels, written in the fifth century on purple-stained vellum. There are only four other such volumes in the world.

Other stops included a night under the fifth century B.C. Temple of Poseidon on Cape Sounion; a brand-new, man-made yacht haven, Vougliameni; and Spetsai, an attractive town near enough to Athens to be used for summer residences. We stopped there for the anniversary of the island's liberation from the Turks. The old American *Thistle* was there, and a new, 200-foot, three-masted sailing ship. In Hydra we tied up stern to the jetty, just before the Saturday night rush. Everybody who is anybody brings his boat to Hydra for Saturday night. The harbor is small, encircled by high cliffs, and very attractive. We had just gotten settled, in a harbor that was already nearly full, when the fleet started to come in. They were all sizes, starting at about 60 feet and getting bigger, motor yachts and sailing vessels alike. I have never seen anything like it before. Some were handled expertly; others, the majority, didn't foul things up too badly. Then there were the rest. I don't know how they found room where they did; some shouldn't have, but that didn't seem to matter.

The noise, we were told, ricochets back and forth between the cliffs well into daylight Sunday; but we weren't staying for the night. As we were clearing our stern lines in preparation for our departure, two boats that had just arrived started for the slot we were about to vacate. They were about the same size, but much larger than *Velila*. We got clear after considerable shouting, placement of fenders, and pushing off, and one engine or another full speed this way or that. Our departure from the tangle only increased the shouting, pushing, and poor boat handling. The boat that had nearly rammed us head on finally took our place. The other one pushed in somewhere else. We got away unscratched and spent a quiet night in a cove all by ourselves.

Two weeks after departing from Rhodes we arrived in Piraeus to unload the charterees. I decided to go directly to Australia.

Fanfare *in Australian waters*

8. Australia

UPON arrival in Sydney, I visited the Cruising Yacht Club of Australia, the club which sponsors the Sydney-Hobart Race. Merv Davey, the club secretary, cordially welcomed me to Australia and set out to arrange my use of the club's facilities during my stay. Soon I found myself being introduced as "Sandy who sailed on *Rabbit.*" There was never any need to explain about *Rabbit.*

The following weekend I found myself on board *Kurura,* a 38-foot sloop, for the Montagu Island Race. It is approximately 350 miles from Sydney south around the island of Montagu and back. While in England I had heard that the winds and seas down in Australia were really tough, that the English Channel was child's play compared to the conditions off Sydney. I'd been in Sydney one week and the wind had varied between a light breeze and non-existent. People the world over have a tendency to remember the extremes as a normal occurrence.

Friday afternoon the wind began to pick up, with a southwest gale forecast for that night. Our start was at 5:00 P.M. We had plenty of ballast, seven on the crew, and an under-rigged boat.

We were late for the start, but the fleet was bothering each other's wind so that we caught up during the short run down Sydney Harbor. It was blowing between 25 and 30 knots. A few boats tried setting spinnakers. They had more trouble than it was worth. Rounding South Head we were in the middle of the fleet. We hardened onto the starboard tack and headed straight out to sea. My watch was off so I went below to get some rest; it looked like a long hard night ahead. The seas had picked up considerably and we were jumping around like a top, but we were still moving well under full mainsail and working jib. I thought we would do better with less main and a larger headsail, but the problem of tying in a reef kept us with full main. It isn't that tying in a reef is so difficult; the problem arises because people don't do it often, or at all, so they don't know the steps to follow. Headsails are taken off and put on all the time, so this becomes easier than trying something new when the going gets rough. Consequently, boats without roller reefing, and some with,

[85]

delay the decision to reduce sail well beyond the proper time. The reefing gear on *Rabbit,* although not perfect, convinced me that roller reefing is the only answer to the problem of shortening the main, whether cruising or racing.

Around 7:00 P.M. I overheard some discussion as to whether we should tack or not. I paid little attention, for this seemed to be a navigational problem, and I didn't have the slightest idea of where we were going. Certainly I had no idea of the tactical strategy of standing offshore or tacking along the coast. As it turned out, the discussion was whether we should tack and return to Sydney or continue in the race.

Because three members of the crew were sick, we headed back for Sydney, spending the night in a sheltered cove east of Manly. Saturday we were slow to rise and sailed in a gentle breeze south along the coast. Everyone was sorry we had withdrawn, but was looking forward to a relaxing weekend on the water.

After that weekend I looked around for work, since *Fanfare* wasn't due for another two months. I landed a temporary job giving away encyclopedias, but I didn't even make it to the first day. At the Ship's Inn, a pub in which a portion is taken over by the yachties each weekday evening, Max Crawford asked if I'd like to fly to Brisbane to bring a boat down to Sydney. He and Garry Wheatley were leaving on the 8:00 P.M. flight. I didn't want to give away encyclopedias anyway; I was back in forty minutes with my sailing gear, ready to go.

The 727 took nearly an hour to fly to Brisbane. The boat, *Winston Churchill,* was located at Norman Wright's Yard. We visited with the Wrights until well into the morning. Norman is an ex-champion of the 18-footers. He has some great pictures of huge masses of sail on practically no boat at all. The 18-foot regulations are rather simple, limiting the hull to 18 feet. A few years ago these 18-foot hulls carried up to 2,000 square feet of sail. Ballast was provided by people and sand bags, either of which might well be discarded overboard during the race. It is no wonder that betting became the Sunday afternoon activity for Sydneyites. They followed the fleet around the course in local ferries, which leaned dangerously as the passengers crowded to one side to watch the progress of these fantastic boats. Eighteen-footers still race, but without the huge spread of canvas.

Eight A.M. and the flooding tide came awfully fast, but we managed to get under way. We powered down the river, and as we were about to enter the new channel through the wide shallow bay outside Brisbane we came to a slow stop on a mud flat. What was going on? We were still in the channel. There was a marker off to port, right where it was supposed to be.

With the tide falling fast we were anxious to get off, but the engine at full speed wasn't enough. All sails were set hurriedly, and with the engine churning up the muddy water and all of us hanging on the main boom we slowly swung around and came off. We got back into the new channel and continued under sail. Now the engine was emitting a strange noise. An investigation revealed that the gear box was badly leaking the hydraulic fluid required to keep the clutch operating properly. The pressure had dropped way down. Nothing we did would get it back up. With a long trip ahead of us, we decided to return to Brisbane for repairs. It was far easier to reach the decision than it was to reach Brisbane, which was almost dead to windward up a busy river dredged to a width of less than 200 yards. The tide was against us and the wind was dying. To make the situation more tense the steering wheel on "Winnie" was hooked up backward. To turn the boat to starboard, you had to turn the wheel counter-clockwise instead of clockwise. We finally made it, in 5 hours. It had taken only one hour to get down the river.

The following morning, with the leak fixed, we were off again. It was fortunate that it was repaired, for the wind was nonexistent all day and throughout the night. We powered south with "George," the automatic pilot, doing most of the steering. He was the only one who didn't get confused by the reversed steering mechanism. Friday we had a great spinnaker run, with the wind dead astern. The helmsman had to stay wide awake to keep from an unexpected gybe. That night we put into Port Stephens for supper at the Country Club Hotel. At midnight Sunday we tied up to the marina in front of the C.Y.C.

That week I joined the railroad staff as a "Goods Assistant." Actually, I was a laborer of the lowest sort, loading and unloading the railroad cars. For the next four weeks I worked during the week and raced on the weekends, with Gordan Ingate on *Caprice of Huon* in the Cabbage Tree Race, which we won, and in a day race in which the entire fleet except for one went around the wrong course. I also joined Bill Fesq for a day race on his "new" boat *Koorna*. Bill had just purchased her and was planning on some changes for the next season. There was plenty of wind throughout the race, picking up to 35 to 40 knots. *Koorna* is under-rigged, so we had hoped for some wind. That we got, and a little extra. During the two windward legs the lifelines were well submerged. Half the fleet retired, so we must have come in in the first half of the starters anyway.

Later, in Mackay, I joined the motor cruiser *Esmerelda* for a three-day cruise of the Barrier Reef. On board I found ten fellow passengers, six of them Americans. The boat was built as a sub chaser during World War II. The four gasoline engines, which then pushed her along at 25 to 30 knots, were since replaced by twin diesels providing a sedate speed of 10 knots. Accommodations have been increased to provide for 24 guests and 4 crew members, and I am sure are greatly improved.

Our first stop was Lindeman Island, a small island in amongst the string just inshore of the Great Barrier Reef. There is a small resort hotel tucked under a cliff, on a nice sandy beach which opens onto a beautiful blue bay. I climbed the three-mile path to the summit, some 700 feet above sea level, for a panoramic view of lush green islands with varicolored blue water forming channels and bays. These open out into the open sea on one side and the Capricorn Channel on the other.

Early the next morning some of the guests from shore joined us for the trip out to the Reef. On the way we stopped at Dent Island and visited the Walches' coral exhibit, well known among coral lovers and museums throughout the world. Bill Walch dives for all the coral and shells that they have collected and then boils the fish life (which is the coloring) off. His wife then paints the correct coloring back on. If they didn't do this, we learned, the fish would die, losing the colors and leaving the smell of dead fish.

Some 50 to 60 miles off the mainland we anchored and went "ashore" onto the coral reef. The reef was just showing and we walked around to look at some of the coral and shells that we had seen at Dent Island. There were lots of clams, mostly 5 or 6 inches long, nowhere near the size of the 400-pounder the Walches had. The Great Barrier Reef, notorious for its dangers from wind and current, is a very interesting formation so far from land. The coral grows at a rate of 8 inches each year. I wonder how long it took to grow to its present state. At some places on the outer edge of the reef the water is over 400 feet deep.

We spent the night anchored off the reef. We returned to Lindeman the next morning. From Lindeman I flew on to Mackay, changed planes, and continued on to Sydney. There I joined *Fanfare*, which had arrived during my absence.

Saturday was her first day sailing in Australian waters. I arrived in time for the afternoon sail Sunday. We had two weeks to get to know the boat, where everything was, and how things worked. The first of two warm-up races we entered was the Middle Harbor Yacht Club's Wednesday afternoon race. The other was the Royal Sydney Yacht Squadron Race from Sydney to Newport at Broken Bay. As the final week of preparation progressed the C.Y.C. became a beehive of activity. Boats were arriving from various parts of Australia. The foreign contingent included boats from England, Italy, South Africa, Hong Kong, and New Zealand.

The biggest attraction was the entry of *Stormvogel,* a 73-foot yawl which had cruised and raced in waters all around the world. The Italian entry was *Corsaro II,* sailed by the Italian Naval Academy. The fleet was the largest ever, drawing a record number of foreign yachts. The race had come of age, not only because it was the 21st running of the Sydney-Hobart, but because it had become accepted

Fanfare's *crew:* (*top row*) *Freddie Thomas, Sandy Weld, Doug Patterson, Len Hedges, Bob Garnham,* (*bottom row*) *Geof Pattinson* (*owner and skipper*), *Gordon Reynolds, Graham Newland*

throughout ocean racing circles as one of the great tests of man, boat, and gear.

In 1945 John Illingworth persuaded a small band of friends who wanted to sail to Hobart to race there. That was the beginning. Nine boats started. One withdrew during the south-southwest gale that scattered the fleet the second day out. All except Illingworth's *Rani* hove to or sought shelter. *Rani,* which was the smallest boat, not only won the race on corrected time, but beat the second boat across the line by some 17 hours.

Now, around the C.Y.C., crews were scraping, rubbing, painting, polishing, sewing, splicing, tuning, checking, and thinking. Old rivalries were renewed and new ones created. A friendly one arose between the crews on *Balandra* and *Fanfare. Balandra* is a sister ship to *Quiver IV,* a member of the successful 1965 English Admiral's Cup team. Eventually a keg was bet on which of us would beat the other. *Balandra* measures 46'2" L.O.A., 35' L.W.L., beam 12', draft

Sydney Harbor

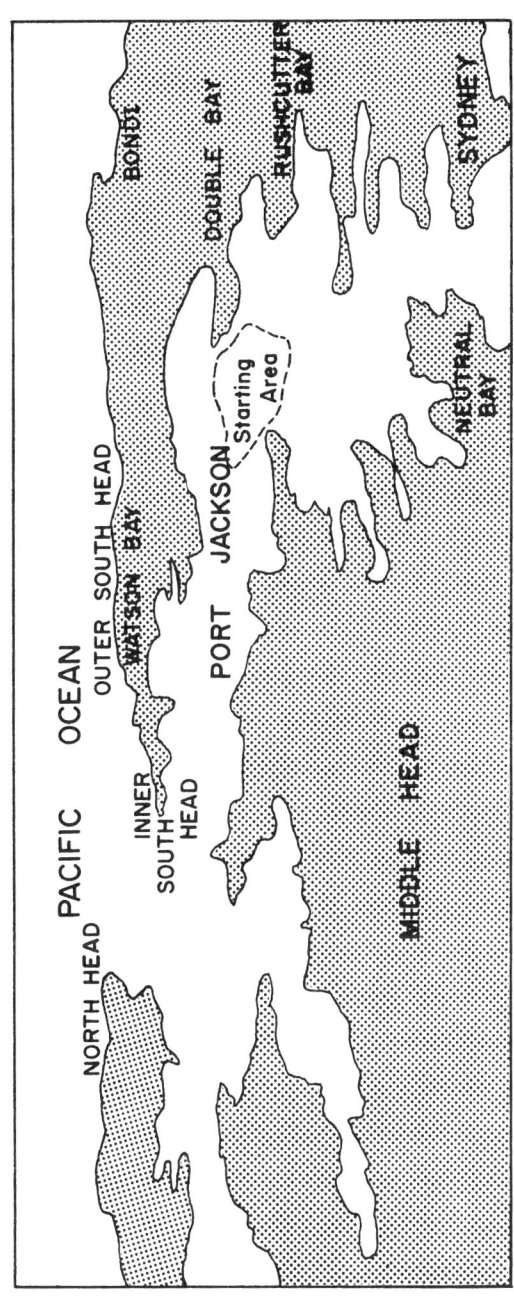

7'6", while *Fanfare* is 48' L.O.A., 35' L.W.L., 11'9" beam, and 7'6" draft. The boats are almost exactly the same size.

Boxing Day, the day of the start, is the day after Christmas and in 1965 fell on a Sunday. The weather was like no other December 26 that I have seen. Santa Claus brings toys on his surfboard down there. This particular Sunday was the most beautiful day imaginable.

The race circular describes the starting area as follows: "From the marshalling area behind the starting line at Clark Island a clear line is left down the harbor, for the racing yachts to sail to the Heads. Patrol boats from the Maritime Service Board, the police and the Volunteer Coastal Patrol maintain this unobstructed area." It goes on to say "At last all [racers] clear the Heads and a procession of yachts has been formed that will be constantly changing all the way to Hobart, and the finish line. But for yachtsmen and spectators alike, the start of the race will be the outstanding spectacle that will be remembered when many other aspects of the race are long forgotten."

It is ironic that the last of this quotation is true at least partly because of the complete inaccuracy of the first portion.

At the start a moderate southeaster provided for a reach down Port Jackson to the Heads. The area behind the starting line had been kept clear, but after the start, with all 50 racers reaching toward the inner South Head, there was no such thing as a clear unobstructed line down the harbor.

On the water, crowded between the starting line and South Head, were literally thousands of boats, some sail, some power, many large, many more very small. There was one thing common to them all: they were loaded with passengers. Laden ferries squeezed as close as they dared. Nearly every cruising-racing boat that wasn't in the race was out to watch the fleet off. Dinghies were everywhere, loaded with young hopefuls testing the speed of their craft against that of the racing fleet. As a matter of fact, nearly anything that could float, from bathtubs and surfboards (one I saw had three people on it) to a passenger liner that tried to make its exit just after our start, was there to follow the fleet down the harbor.

Sydney–Hobart Race

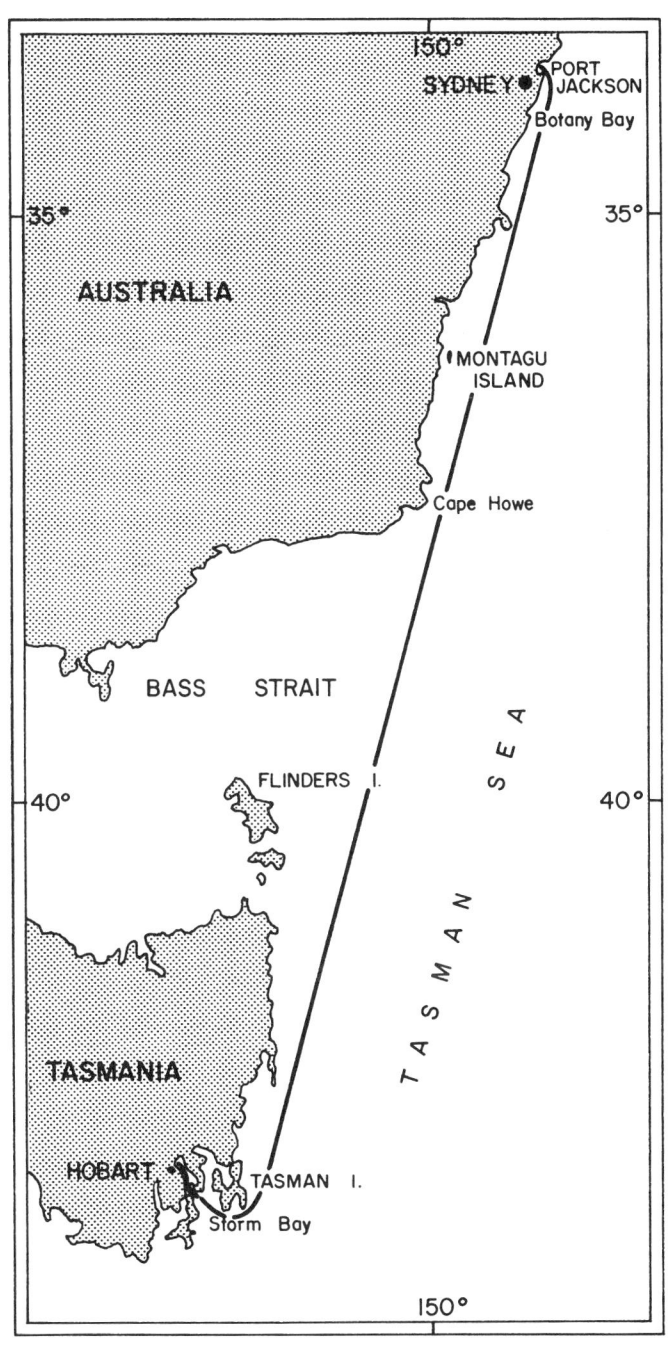

Nor were the spectators only on the water. The points and bays along our course that form Port Jackson were now fuzzy from skyline to waterline with spectators who waved and shouted encouragement as the boats surged past. There were even planes overhead, not very far from the mastheads. The largest group of spectators was still at home watching TV. Movie and live television cameras had been set up at every possible point, on shore, on boats, and in the air, to allow those unable to get to Sydney the opportunity of seeing this brilliant and colorful spectacle.

We got a good start in the middle of the line with clear air. *Stormvogel* played it cautiously, being further to leeward and 150 yards from the line when the gun fired. It didn't take her long to close the gap and she led the fleet past the South Heads. How she made it I'm not sure, for there were two dozen small boats anchored right off the rocks at this point. As there is deep water in very close and the point is a distinct turning mark, the whole fleet was converging on it at a speed of 7 to 8 knots. *Stormvogel* threaded her way through without incident. *Corsaro II* got halfway through the mess before running over a small boat. Upon seeing this mass of hulls and sails converging on them, the crew of the small boat had decided to pull up their anchor and move. *Corsaro II* had to swing around another small boat, and headed for the spot the runabout was moving into as it pulled in its long anchor line. The runabout and *Corsaro II* each made unexpected moves toward the other, and met at the same spot in the water. *Corsaro II* hardly slowed down. The runabout was swamped, with no one hurt, apparently, as they waved *Corsaro II* on.

Enid and *Fanfare* followed on *Stormvogel*'s heels around the inner South Head. We were closely followed by *Balandra* and *Corsaro II*. Then came the rest of the fleet, weaving back and forth like drunken sailors, trying to avoid colliding with the spectators.

Yes, that start is one I will remember for a long, long time!

Once clear of the Heads we settled down to serious sailing, hard on the wind. Soon we had edged to windward of the fleet. The tack closest to our rhumb line was the port tack, down the coast, not quite fetching the easternmost points. On that tack we were riding the seas more easily. But the tactical move, many believe, is to get off the coast to pick up the southerly set. Who knows which tack would be the best one for this race? The afterguard decided that we would head along the coast for a while. Geof, who had participated in two previous Sydney-Hobart Races, has always wanted to get away from the coast, but has never been able to.

That evening we crossed tacks with *Stormvogel,* which pleased us considerably. She then stood out to sea. We went inshore and sat becalmed for several hours. In the morning we discovered *Bacchus D* right ahead of us. We were disappointed; she is not considered particularly fast.

The course record was set in 1962 by Huey Long's globe-trotting *Ondine,* when she enjoyed a hull-speed reach and later a sleigh-ride run all the way to Storm Bay, and shattered the old course record set by *Kurrewa IV* in 1957 by 14 hours, 44 minutes, and 13 seconds. In doing so, the 57-foot *Ondine* and the 38-year-old schooner *Astor* (73 feet) staged a dramatic finish line duel.

After a fast passage, *Astor* put the brakes on under Cape Raoul in Storm Bay. Slatting forlornly, she had to wait some 6 hours before *Ondine* rounded Tasman Island. With her modern rig and light sails *Ondine* closed to within a mile of *Astor* before she started to move again. *Ondine* hugged the shore, gybing back and forth, to stay out of whatever current there was, while the deep-drafted *Astor* sailed up the middle of the Derwent River with her huge venturi spinnaker. With about 8 miles to go, *Astor* was forced to run dead downwind and her "gollywobbler" ceased to draw. *Ondine,* well inshore, gybed and crept ahead. Rounding the last point with a short way to go, *Astor* began to close the gap as the breeze freshened. *Ondine* drifted over the line a mere minute ahead. Her elapsed time was 3 days, 3 hours, 46 minutes, and 16 seconds. For those on shore the excitement must have been great, but it couldn't have been anything compared to that on the two boats.

Conditions in 1965 weren't quite the same as they were in 1962. We weren't about to break any records. Monday, Tuesday, and all day Wednesday we had light running or reaching conditions. For

Bacchus D *with spinnaker problems. Note crew in top half of the spinnaker trying to unwrap it from the headstay.*

most of Tuesday we couldn't leave *Camelot* (L.O.A. 36'8", L.W.L. 30') behind. Wednesday night the wind picked up strength from the north, giving us quite a ride down the Tasmanian Coast. The wind was dead astern and steering became tense, not only because of the seas, but also due to poor visibility. The sky was pitch black, without moon or stars. We had a big dark blue spinnaker up which was next to impossible to see.

The wind subsided as we continued down the coast Thursday morning. Lunch was postponed a few minutes as we rounded Tasman Island, hardening up for the 40-mile reach across Storm Bay to the entrance to the Derwent River. Actually lunch was never served. As soon as we got under Tasman Light we were blasted by 35 to 40 knots of wind whooping down from the top of Tasman Island. Over *Fanfare* went on her side, water pouring into the cockpit. I reached under water for the spinnaker sheet. Slackening it helped to collapse the sail. But I wasn't out of trouble. The sheet was too short; I'd run out of rope and had to take all but two turns off the winch. As we righted and began to bear off, the chute filled with an explosion. The initial shock took the sheet out of my hands. The knot on the end didn't even hesitate as it reached the block on the transom that the sheet was led through. It just pulled it cleanly off the deck. The sheet, somehow detaching itself from the spinnaker, landed in the water some 80 yards away.

It was a struggle to get the spinnaker down and the genoa up, but we accomplished it without mishap. Fifteen minutes later we were once again under spinnaker and staysail in a light northerly. These conditions lasted for about 30 minutes, just time enough to get the gear straightened out, before a line squall hit us. We didn't go all the way over this time, but we definitely wanted the spinnaker off. The only sensible way to do this was to bear off before the wind, but *Fanfare* wouldn't respond to the rudder, even though the wheel was hard over. As I waited on the foredeck it seemed like hours, but it was undoubtedly not much over 5 minutes before she bore away.

With the #2 genoa up this time we still had too much sail on. It was time for a few rolls in the main. With five of us on the foredeck (I was cleaning up the spinnaker gear) and around the mast it took nearly 5 minutes of discussion to start the simple task. Geof, who was standing in the companionway hatch watching and waiting, turned to Graham who was steering and said "What we need up there is a few more Indians and less chiefs." How true; that's one of the major problems of sailing on strange boats with different shipmates. The task was finally accomplished.

Once past the Raoul the wind eased again, allowing us to go back to full sail. Later it swung into the west, allowing us to just fetch the "Iron Pot," the sentinel that marks the entrance to the Derwent River. If the west wind spread, the fleet behind would have a beat all the way in from Tasman Island. We could see some boats well astern, and they were being headed badly. But where were *Balandra, Stormvogel,* and the other hot boats?

The 12 miles up the Derwent River to the finish line often present crews with a certain amount of frustration, due to the fickle winds and tidal currents. Many yachts have spent a night becalmed at the river's mouth, allowing the rest of the fleet to catch up. We didn't have it that way. Our wind indicator registered 30 knots as we drove up the river hard on the wind under full sail. What amazed me most was that *Fanfare*'s lee rail didn't even get wet.

We crossed the finish line off Battery Point at 7:00 P.M. amidst a cheering crowd. Traditionally the townsfolk of Hobart greet each competing boat, right down to the very last, with a tumultuous welcome. More noise greeted us as we entered Constitution Dock and tied up. We were fourth to finish; *Stormvogel, Balandra,* and *Freya* were already in. That night the wind wasn't typical on the Derwent; it continued fresh. I joined the crowd welcoming the boats in throughout the night, with most of the fleet in by nine o'clock the next morning. The eventual winner was *Freya,* picking up a coveted Hat Trick, her third consecutive Sydney-Hobart win. On corrected time we came in fifth in our division and eleventh in the fleet. That wasn't too bad, but it wasn't what we had hoped for, especially since *Balandra* beat us.

Later that afternoon, as I was returning to *Fanfare,* I saw Freddie

Freddie Thomas, the keg, Bob Creighton-Brown, Sandy Weld

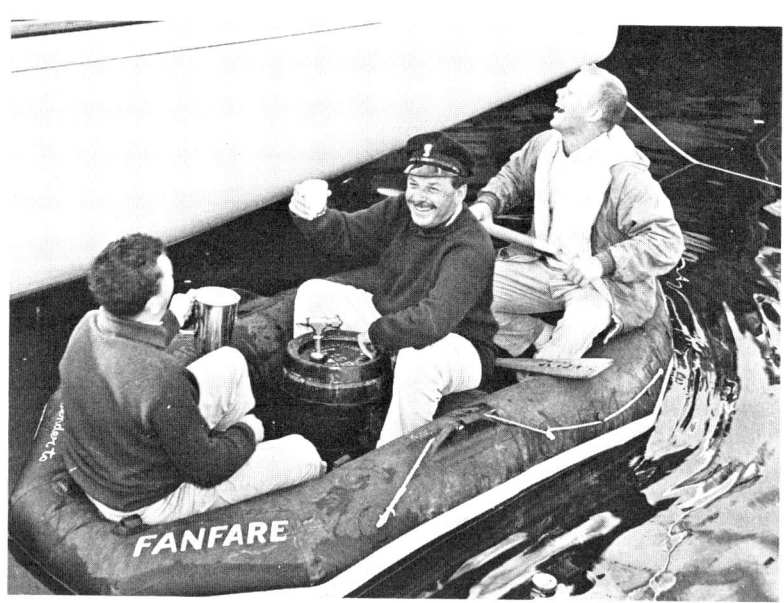

and the younger members of *Balandra*'s crew with long faces. Bob Creighton-Brown, *Balandra*'s owner, wouldn't allow the keg on board. We couldn't blame him, for we didn't want any of the obviously resulting mess on *Fanfare* either. The final stumbling block was a local law forbidding opening it on the dock. So, with an untapped keg waiting to be emptied, ingenuity had to take over.

Freddie and I pumped up *Fanfare*'s Avon rubber dinghy and paddled over to *Balandra*. In went the keg. Then, after considerable persuasion, Bob Creighton-Brown (an insurance man in Sydney) joined Freddie and me for a spin around Constitution Dock and the ceremonial tapping of the keg. He was rather sceptical about the whole episode, especially his being in the dinghy with us, but we got him back to shore not only safe but dry as well. Then we loaded up with five of *Balandra*'s younger members. That made seven of us in the dinghy plus the keg; it didn't leave much freeboard. As we pushed off, Bob Creighton-Brown was heard saying, "I wouldn't underwrite that voyage for anything in the world!" We weren't concerned, for there was hardly a ripple on the water inside the Dock.

But it wasn't long before George Sullens, one of the crew off *Seawind,* went along the Dock taking bets on whether or not he could sink us. He drummed up a lot of enthusiasm for his scheme, but not many bettors. It turned out that he got only two, Graham Newland and Gordon Reynolds, both off *Fanfare*! Fine shipmates they were.

George and a mate of his dove in after us. To keep ourselves in relative safety we handed our would-be attackers a paper cup half full of beer. This stopped their attack. But the crowd along the dock didn't like that. There were catcalls of "Bribery!" and "Sink them!" It seemed that they wanted us sunk—or at least themselves part of the party. A dozen sporadic splashes were heard from all sides of the dock as people dove in to join the party. We held them off for a while, until they began to get cold and we ran out of cups. Our warnings to them not to get excited because of the keg on board kept the dinghy right side up, but not altogether dry.

The solution seemed to be to get the keg on board *Seawind* (her crew must have been well represented there). Then we would allow them to sink us—that is, if we didn't beat the keg onto *Seawind.* As the keg was being lifted on board, too many eager hands, either reaching for the keg or trying to evacuate the dinghy before completely joining the rest in the water, caused a few people, followed by the keg, to topple overboard. Much to everyone's surprise it floated, and was hoisted immediately on board and finished. No rescue could have been performed with any greater speed and finesse than that one.

9. Thar She Blows

FANFARE left Hobart early Tuesday morning without me. I had a ride to New Zealand with Allen Adams on his 33-foot *Tairere* bound for Auckland. It is a passage of some 1,500 miles, far greater than I had imagined from looking at any globe.

We were ready to depart Tuesday morning, but the "donk" (as New Zealanders call an engine) wouldn't start. All afternoon a mechanic worked on it as we sat around cooling our heels. At 4:45 P.M., quitting time, the engine ran smoothly. We were off by five o'clock.

A hundred yards outside the dock the engine stopped of its own accord. We hoisted sail and continued on. The wind was very light and from the southeast. It took us over 36 hours to pass Tasman Light, a distance of 46 miles. Our speed would surely improve; the Tasman Sea is notorious for its southwest gales. We were expecting a fast trip to Auckland, less than 10 days. At sunrise the second morning out, land was still visible astern. The wind stayed light out of the south the whole way across. We had the spinnaker up most of the time. One day we rolled off 167 miles from noon to noon. Otherwise, each noon reading was about 100 miles further to the east.

One evening while I was on deck alone, as we sailed along on a placid sea, our keel hit something. The momentum of the hull, as we rocked forward, carried us over the obstacle. My instant thought was "How did that sand bar get way out here and why hasn't it been found before?" Land wasn't within hundreds of miles in any direction, and the water was supposed to be 2,000 feet deep. As these thoughts flashed through my mind I looked behind us. There, just sliding back beneath the surface, was the back of a whale! Those below were out of their bunks and on deck with amazing speed. (They saw the whale's tail too.) We had actually scraped the back of this mammal as it was heading south for the mating grounds, with other thoughts on its mind.

That wasn't the only whale we saw. The next afternoon I saw a large one steaming south just on the surface, about 100 yards away. We were on a converging course. I couldn't head higher to go be-

[101]

hind it without taking in the spinnaker; maybe the whale would sound and leave us alone. It blew every now and then as it continued along undisturbed. I was alone on deck again, but a "Thar she blows" brought everyone on deck with the same speed as the day before. There were a few anxious minutes as we crossed in front of the whale. Later on, three more were spotted travelling together.

The thought crossed our minds that these animals were terribly hard to see, even in daylight. How close had we come to others during the night? They didn't seem to notice us at all, but we were anxious to keep at a comfortable distance. They are a good deal larger than *Tairere,* and by all tales pack a tremendous punch.

The shortest day's run was 40 miles. We spent 6 hours during this day competely becalmed. All sails were lowered and as it was 10:00 P.M. everyone went to bed.

It was a strange night; the atmosphere was heavy. It couldn't be called fog, and there wasn't really a haze. The sky was total blackness, no stars or moon. One could hardly tell the difference between water and sky. Nor was there a breath of wind.

I'd just climbed into my bunk when I heard what I thought to be a whale blowing. I didn't want to believe it. But as it continued to blow and was obviously getting closer, it was more and more clearly a whale. Up on deck again we couldn't see a thing, but we certainly could hear him, coming directly at us! There was little we could do. We couldn't move the boat, for there was no wind and the engine still wasn't working. Just as I expected to see him hit us amidships the blowing ceased. He was apparently alerted by the vibrations caused by our slight rocking. After a few more minutes of listening, we returned to our bunks.

Because of the slow passage we began to run low on food before sighting New Zealand. We trailed a hook and line most of the time, catching only two tuna. They weren't particularly tasty, but disappeared without complaint from any of us. Allen promised that we would catch some kingfish off North Cape.

One morning the Three Kings were sighted off to port and North Cape dead ahead. We sailed in close to the rugged coast. Along the shore of Spirits Bay a fishing trawler named *Provider* came alongside offering some crayfish. We didn't hesitate a second in accepting, and traded five huge crayfish for some Cascade Beer, Hobart's best. The fish were so big that only one would fit in the large pot at one time. Three were cooked before the cooking methyl alcohol ran out. We didn't starve, for they were ample for one meal.

The next day we entered Whangaroa Harbor, a 5-mile-long sound with few inhabitants along its tree-covered perimeter. At a small settlement nestled on its shore, we purchased supplies, fixed the engine, cooked the two remaining crayfish, and cleared customs.

The wind continued light or non-existent as we ghosted down the east coast, powering as long as the gasoline supply lasted. A pleasant spinnaker run on the last afternoon was the best sailing we had had in over 5 days. Our passage to Auckland took 14 days and 4 hours. It was a pleasant crossing, one few people would have believed possible in the stormy Tasman Sea.

Flying from New Zealand via Tahiti and Hawaii, I arrived in Boston during the second week in March. The next project was to prepare *Safari,* a 39-foot Concordia yawl, for the 1966 Bermuda Race.

More time is spent in preparing for the Bermuda Race than the Fastnet or Sydney-Hobart. The Bermuda Race, held early in June, is at the very opening of the sailing season in the northeastern United States. Consequently owners, crews, wives, and their friends start planning during the bitter cold winter months. Everything is planned "from soup to nuts," and the preparation continues right up to the moment when the boats push off for the starting line. On the other hand, the Fastnet Race more or less climaxes the R.O.R.C. season, and the Sydney-Hobart is at the peak of the Australian season. We had had only one day in which to prepare *Rabbit* for the Fastnet Race itself, and the two weeks we had to prepare *Fanfare* for the Sydney-Hobart were certainly ample. However, *Safari*'s season was still ahead of her, and this was reflected in the preparations.

The 1966 race was the 25th to Bermuda in a series that dates back to 1906. The fleet of 167 boats had a bright clear day for the start off Newport, Rhode Island, with a light southwesterly. The race was

Bermuda Race

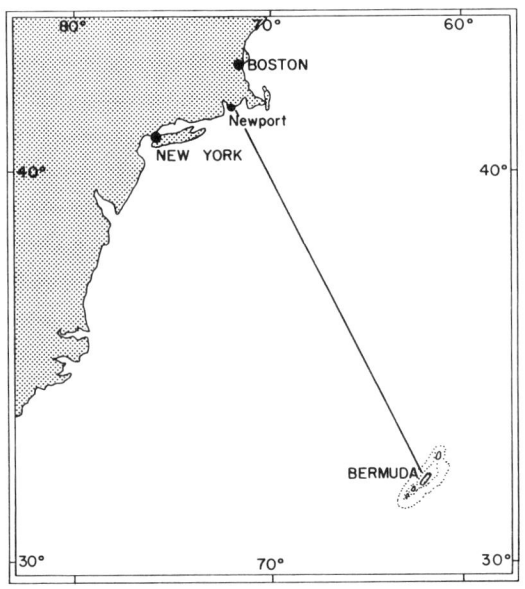

more or less uneventful right down to the last few miles from the finish. The first boats in had light variable conditions, but then things changed. They changed so much so that old timers were heard to say that it was one of the toughest Bermuda Races ever sailed.

After the boats had peacefully crossed the Gulf Stream, squalls could be seen in the distance Thursday morning approaching the majority of the becalmed fleet. They had started building up over Bermuda the previous evening just as *Kialoa* was becoming first-to-finish, followed by the new *Palawan*.

Two events disturbed our otherwise uneventful race to the Onion Patch. Just before evening on the night we hoped to enter the Gulf Stream, assuming our navigator could find it, we changed from a shy spinnaker to the #1 genoa. In the change, I lost the snap shackle end of the spinnaker halyard and had the awful feeling of seeing it swing halfway up the mast. The next 45 minutes were spent trying to retrieve the halyard. A pyramid of people and the boathook could just reach it, but to hook it was beyond hope. It wasn't going to wait for us either; it quickly swung around to leeward of the mast and main and got tangled in the backstay, where it promptly wound itself up tight.

Having no spare halyards from aloft we were all right for the time, but with night approaching and anything possible in the Stream it was deemed wise to retrieve it. Since I had been the culprit to cause the problem, I was hoisted aloft. It was a surprisingly pleasant trip up the windward side of the mast as we reached along under main and mizzen. That was until I reached the top and looked down. I then found myself out over the water with a very small deck far below.

The next day, in bright blue water, with cloudless sky and little wind, a herd of whales passed close by, lazing along on the surface. Some passed closer than others. Two, side by side, were headed on a collision course with our beam. My uncle, who was on the helm, wouldn't alter course. Neither did the whales. As the two lovers approached, cameras came out of various corners of the boat. Finally, leaving hardly a ripple in the water, they submerged some 10 feet from us.

One of the photographers had a movie camera. The resulting film was an amusing display of his growing excitement as the whales approached. He not only forgot to change from telephoto to normal lens, he forgot to release the shutter. The last part of the film was a collage of quick glimpses of whales' heads, water, deck, sky, sail, and his feet.

Thursday was spent drifting into squalls and making fine speed on course for 10 to 15 minutes. Gradually we would be headed and would finally have to tack as the breeze moderated steadily down to nothing. Each squall was different. In some there was driving rain with winds up to 35 to 40 m.p.h.; others had the rain and no wind. Sail changing and navigation became frustrating. The wind's strength varied so widely and quickly that it was impossible to keep up with it.

Thursday evening the wind picked up to 40 to 50 knots and held. We went through the well-prepared but seldom-tried exercise of tying in a reef, and under #3 genoa beat our way in to Bermuda. We arrived Friday afternoon tired, wet, and very happy to be in.

Everyone had his story to tell. Some had been luckier than others. One boat had been plugging to windward Friday morning in blinding sheets of rain 4 miles from the finish line. By mid-afternoon, still hard at it, they were 12 miles from the line, for an average speed of minus one knot. At this point they called it quits and turned on the engine. Under both sail and power they were still making sternway, so they called the Coast Guard. Within the hour they were under tow, finally making headway for St. George's.

The whole fleet was saddened to learn upon arriving in Bermuda of the death of one of America's most colorful and popular sailors, DeCoursey Fales. He had sailed his well-known schooner *Nina* in the Block Island Race only a few weeks previously and had her entered in the Bermuda Race in which she started the day before his death. The commodore had sailed *Nina,* which he referred to as the "Old Lady," in ten Bermuda Races. His biggest victory came in 1962 when he won the Bermuda Trophy, given to the boat with the best corrected time. That was the first time in 32 years the trophy had been won by a schooner, and it was without question the Bermuda Trophy's most popular winner.

A novel feature of the 1966 race was the method of calculating the corrected times. The system was designed to relate a boat's performance to its own rating, based on the average speed of the boats in its class. The intent was to wipe out supposed inequities which made it "impossible" for boats of one size range to win under the given conditions of a particular race. To perform these calculations an I.B.M. computer was used. The results had to wait until 75% of the finish times of each of the six classes had been recorded. These established a speed curve just for this race. Then each boat's rating and speed had to be matched to the speed curve to determine the placings. *Thunderbird,* T.V. Learson's Cal 40, came the farthest above the curve in relation to her rating and was declared the winner; the Argentinian *Nike,* designed by German Frers, was second.

The Onion Patch Trophy was competed for by teams from Argentina, Bermuda, Britain, Germany, and the U.S. The British team of *Noryema IV, Firebrand,* and *Assegai II* cleaned up. It is significant that these boats won under the C.C.A. rule although handicapped by being designed under the R.O.R.C. rules. Perhaps the two rules are not as far apart as some people like to think.

After a weekend of resting and drying out, we headed *Safari* north for her home port on Cape Cod. We started one day before the 42-boat Transatlantic fleet left Bermuda on the 3400-mile race to Skagen Light on Denmark's northern tip. The occasion was the 100th anniversary of the Royal Danish Yacht Club, with the main objective a trophy donated by the King of Denmark. While this fleet met a howling northeast gale off Bermuda, we moseyed along with fine conditions. During the 6-day trip we were forced to don foul weather gear only twice, to keep the dew off.

Within 24 hours of setting foot on Cape Cod, I was airborne for Copenhagen for the second One Ton Cup on a new Carter creation—*Tina*.

Tina *on the heels of* Robin

10. *Tina*

WHILE I was somewhere down under, Edward Stettinius had told Dick he wanted a new boat—a family cruising boat that would hold her own for an occasional R.O.R.C. race. Since the discussed size was about right for the One Ton series and it had seemed like so much fun the previous year in Le Havre, he decided to enter the 1966 series in Copenhagen.

On the surface this seems to be a contradiction in requirements, but there is an obvious correlation. Whether racing or cruising, speed is necessary for the least possible effort. *Tina*'s basis became maximum speed for minimum energy.

As the second boat off Carter's boards, *Tina* had obviously evolved from *Rabbit*. *Rabbit* was an out-and-out ocean racer with everything geared to pure boat speed rather than to close-winded performance. Our experience in Le Havre proved this type of boat to be unsuited to One Ton racing; otherwise the concepts behind *Rabbit* had been quite successful. *Tina* was a windward version.

Tina's downwind running characteristics were de-emphasized by moving some of the displacement further aft in an attempt to get better windward performance. The most obvious change was her maximum draft keel. The trailing edge of the high aspect ratio keel and trim tab sloped forward, providing a new exposure to the hull's aft underbody.

Tina's rig took another step forward from *Rabbit*'s. More sail was placed in the foretriangle, with the same small high aspect ratio main. There are many advantages to a small highly efficient mainsail with its short boom; *Tina*'s boom measured only 12 feet long. The pendulum effect of the boom is reduced and the general handling and furling of the sail is much easier. The importance of being able to reduce sail quickly in order to maintain maximum speed is all too often overlooked. *Tina*'s wineglass-shaped hull shouldn't be sailed over a 25-degree angle of heel for her best speed.

The spar was as clean as possible and along the same lines as *Rabbit*'s. But it had its own experimental features as well. The walls of

Tina

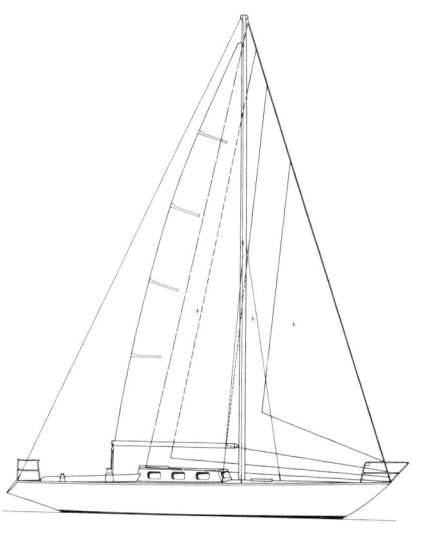

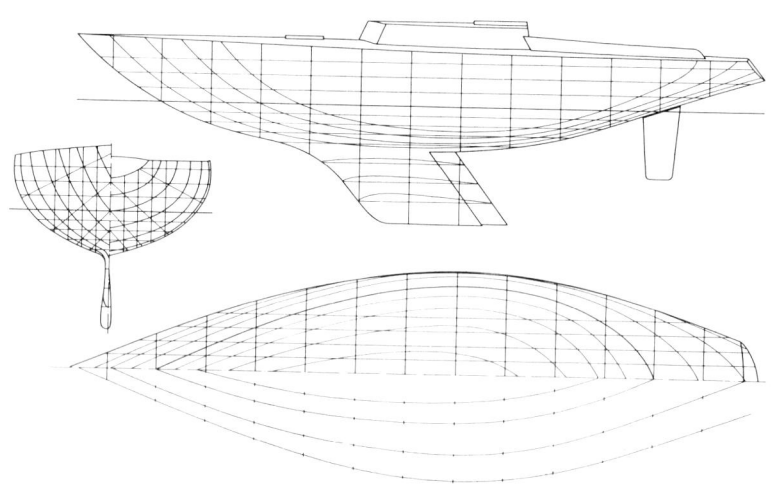

Rabbit, Tina

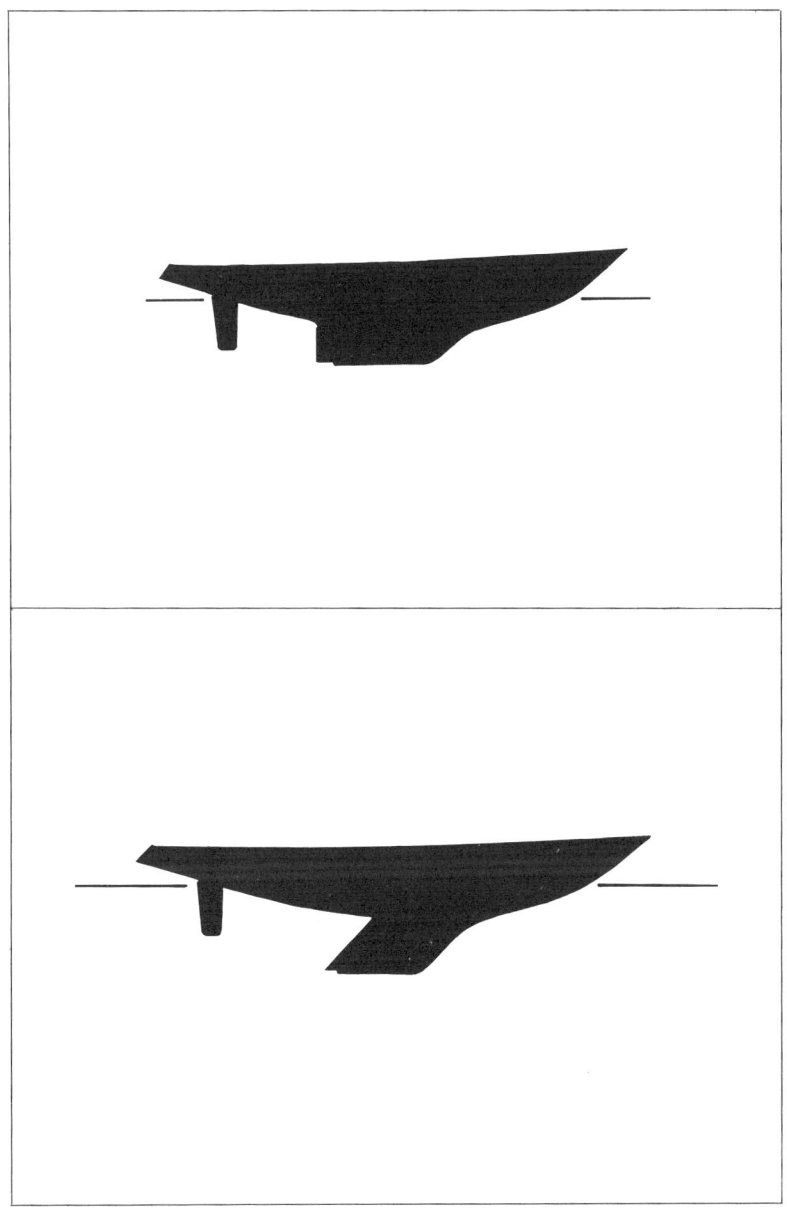

Tina's *roller reefing gear*
Tina *on the ways in Copenhagen* (Below)

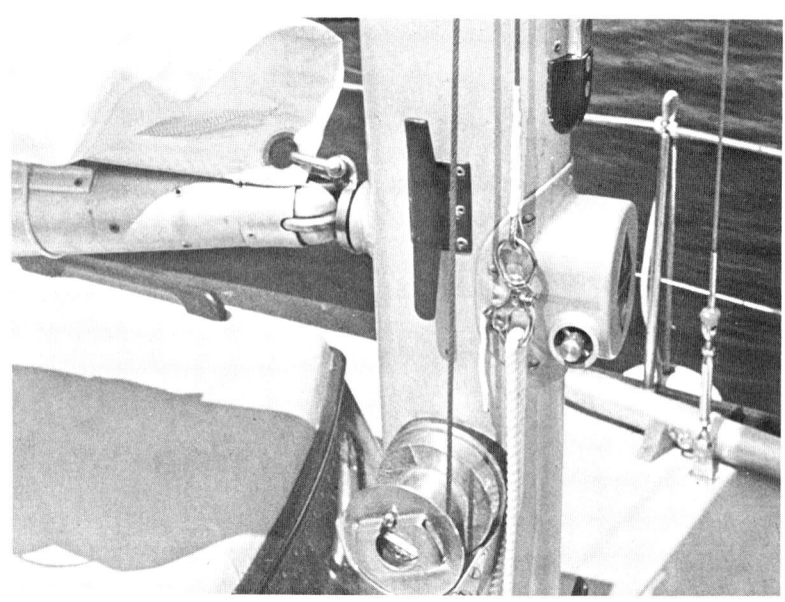

Rabbit's aluminum spar were fairly thick, a feature of strength, but one which gave considerable weight aloft. In an attempt to reduce the thickness of the walls, and thus the weight, Sparlight engineered the spar with internal reinforcings.

A novel feature of *Tina*'s spar was her roller reefing gear, which was a development of *Rabbit*'s. On *Rabbit* it was a one-man job to reef the main, but a two-man job to unreef; an extra pair of hands was required to feed the luff back into the luff groove. In an attempt to eliminate this, *Tina*'s roller reefing gear was placed in front of the mast, and was connected to the boom by a rod through the mast to a universal joint. This eliminated the roller reefing setback altogether and permitted the luff of the mainsail to feed easily into the luff groove.

The One Ton Cup concept had caught the imagination of sailors throughout the world. The 1965 series had been a tremendous success. The 1966 series began to take on international prestige as the best in "offshore" racing. Everyone involved in ocean racing wanted to be there; the best sailors, designers, and sailmakers recognized this series as the testing and proving ground for boats of the future.

When *Tina* was hauled out at Copenhagen for a scrubbing she attracted a good deal of attention, as did the other boats when hauled. One of the internationally-known designers was seen looking at *Tina*'s aft underbody and shaking his head. He was overheard saying, "Dick has himself a lemon this time," implying that *Tina* wouldn't be competitive.

He could have been right; we didn't know. We had sailed straight from launching in Breskens to Copenhagen, never sailing with anyone to get a feel for *Tina*'s relative speed. She seemed easy, a little too easy and quiet. There was no fuss or disturbance as she moved through the water. Did this indicate speed or slowness? It was a little unnerving that she didn't sound or feel "normal."

All competing boats were required to report to the Skovshoved Yacht Club at least three days prior to the first race. All the boats had named berths, side by side in the man-made harbor, within inches of the main thoroughfare of the docking area. The boats drew a great many onlookers, both local people and participants looking over competitive gear and boats. The atmosphere wasn't nearly as cordial as it had been at Le Havre. This year's effort was being taken much more seriously. Part of this was due to an increased number of professional people taking part. In Le Havre, van de Stadt was the only person participating whose business was involved with this type of boat. Dick was merely an amateur designer in 1965 and wasn't included in the professional group. Neither was he in 1966. It took certain members of the sailing world several years to accept the fact that he was anything but an amateur designer who had had one or two lucky breaks.

In 1966, there were seven designer-sailed boats. They were *Tina*, *Robin* (Ted Hood), *Yeoman XIV* (Peter Nicholson), *Tikerak* (Frans Maas), *Aladdin* (van de Stadt), *Salome* (R. Swanson), and *Goodwin* (W. Draüe). André Nelis, a Dutch sailmaker, was sailing *De Schelde*.

Also indicative of the serious attitude was the large number of new boats designed for this series and the large fleets several countries had for trials. England, for example, had had 11 boats actively try out for the three-position team. Nine of these were brand new, designed with the One Ton very much in mind. Two of the selected boats, *Roundabout* and *Clarionet*, were from the boards of Sparkman and Stephens. The other was of Peter Nicholson's design and was sailed by Peter himself. France held two selection trials, one in Le Havre and one in the Mediterranean, so keen was the interest there. Ron Swanson shipped his *Salome* and crew all the way from Australia. There were 27 entries, with 24 boats making it to Copenhagen. The impact of the first series had been world-wide. Gordon Ingate—upon returning to Australia after his superlative performance with *Caprice* in the 1965 Admiral's Cup—put up a cup in Australia for the boat of One Ton Cup size (22-foot rating) with the best record for three specified races.

The developments in *Tina*'s spar caused us several problems, due primarily to transatlantic communications. Two of these concerned the boom's tack and outhaul fittings. They were not recessed into the boom far enough to allow the foot of the mainsail to lie in a straight line between the groove and the fittings. To increase our problems, the mainsail was cut much too full in the lower part of the luff.

It was out of the question to get anything major done; there was neither time nor the facility. There was no way to change the boom fittings. Ted Hood was there, but he was busy readying his own boat for the same series. There were also local sailmakers who could do it. That wouldn't really solve the problem, for the raised fittings would cause further trouble when rolling in a reef.

Yankee ingenuity produced an acceptable compromise. Off came the boom's tack fitting, and we lashed the tack directly to the top of the universal joint. For the clew we took the slide off completely and lashed the clew to the boom with a sail stop, making it next to impossible to adjust the tension along the foot. To eliminate some of the extra fullness in the luff we wrapped a towel around the forward end of the boom and universal joint. This made the diameter larger than that of the boom itself. Then we rolled one turn in the main, thus eliminating much of the sail's fullness. A Cunningham cringle two feet up the leach from the tack could be used to haul down on that part of the sail should we want a really flat sail.

The three days prior to the racing were busy for everyone: the participants, the Race Committee, the measurers, and the Skovshoved Club. All sails that might be used had to be measured, regardless of when they had been measured before. Then each boat's rating was recalculated, just to insure that no boat rated over the 22-foot limit. The boats were checked out completely to insure that they had the proper equipment and complied with the requirement rules. One boat, *Goodwin,* discovered that her headroom did not meet the requirement of the 8-meter cruiser-racer rule. Her crew undertook to lower the cabin floor to comply with the rule. Their task was all the harder because of her steel construction.

Almost everyone went out practicing, even though most of the boats had been sailing for two to three months that summer already with the same crew. We went out as often as we could, for we needed just plain sailing experience on *Tina.* She was to have been out of the yard just one week on the day of the first race.

One Ton Boats

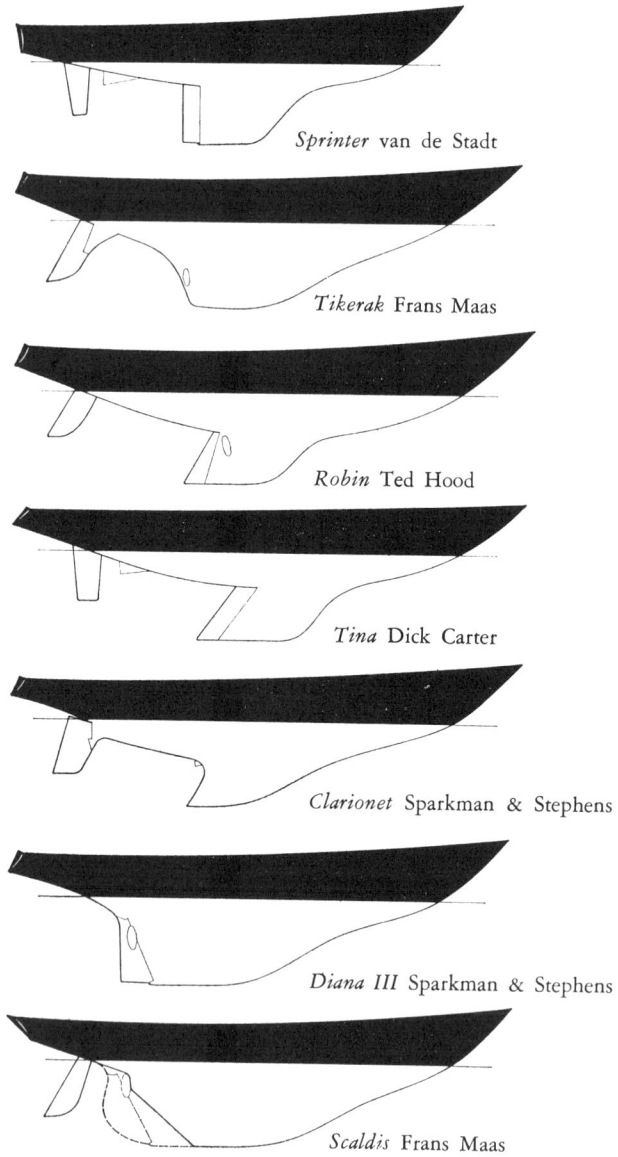

Sprinter van de Stadt

Tikerak Frans Maas

Robin Ted Hood

Tina Dick Carter

Clarionet Sparkman & Stephens

Diana III Sparkman & Stephens

Scaldis Frans Maas

The third U.S. boat, *Shearwater,* was shipped over from Stamford, Connecticut. She was a Hood design and had been extremely successful the previous summer around Long Island. But, due to an error in calculating or measuring *Shearwater*'s rating in the U.S., it was discovered in Copenhagen that she actually rated well above the 22-foot limit. Time was too short to tackle the problem correctly. The mainsail was simply reduced enough to get her rating down to the required 22 feet. Consequently she raced the series with a pitifully small main. Several times the wind velocity was just wrong for her, forcing her to drop the main altogether rather than change to the #2 genoa and be without adequate driving sail. This situation made the tremendous effort, time, and expense already put into the campaign seem like a considerable waste. *Shearwater*'s experience is a prime example of the drastic need for one stable international rating rule.

One of the underlying purposes of the One Ton Cup in 1965, I believe, was to make ocean racing more like one-design racing. It accomplished this in only one respect, that of specifying a rating that one could not exceed. The hulls themselves were as varied in construction, design, and weight as could be imagined. *Robin,* Ted Hood's One Tonner, weighed nearly twice as much as *De Schelde,* also designed for this particular race. The waterline lengths varied from 24.4 feet to 27.4 feet. Overall lengths varied even more, from 31.8 feet for van de Stadt-designed *Playmate* to Hood-designed *Robin* at 38 feet. The ratings were considerably closer, with the Swedish *Ian XIV* the one exception, rating at 21.22. The 23 remaining boats measured in between 21.85 for *Roundabout* to exactly 22.00 for *Sprinter, Malabar,* and *Maryca,* two at 21.99, five at 21.98, *Tina* at 21.96, and *Robin* at 21.88.

Almost all of the new boats featured the fin keel and separate spade rudder. This was a marked departure from the meter boat development that had influenced ocean racers for a number of years. The meter boats don't race under ocean racing conditions, and ocean racers influenced by meter boat design often experienced great difficulties in reaching and downwind steering. The solution appears to be to separate the rudder and keel. Some boats used a skeg in front of the rudder, others didn't. Who made use of the concept first I don't know. Van de Stadt has been designing boats with separated keel and rudder for years. *Stormvogel* was perhaps his most famous ocean racing boat of that type. In the United States the Cal 40 became a very successful class on both the east and west coasts. Then in 1968 *Intrepid,* the United States defender and eventual winner of the America's Cup, appeared with a near fin keel, trim tab, and spade rudder. Was ocean racing influencing 12-meter design?

Race Day arrived quickly. On board *Tina* were Ed Stettinius, Dick and John Carter, and I. Sammy Sampson had signed on a week before in Breskens. Donald Pye was pulled from his bunk, unshaven and without breakfast, the morning of the first race after transportation problems delayed the arrival of our sixth member.

The first race was a 30-miler, laid out in a fine Olympic-shaped course in the Sound. The first leg was a short beat from the starting line in the middle of the circle to the perimeter. *Yeoman* reached the mark first, just ahead of *Ian XIV, Diana III, Roundabout, Robin,* and *Tina.* The following close reach gave an indication of what was to come. *Robin* and *Tina* moved up to first and second, followed closely by *Roundabout.* The ensuing two legs, a run and a beat, saw *Tina* move into the lead and then relinquish it to *Roundabout.* She was some 5 minutes ahead at the last leeward mark. We were in fourth position running down to that mark. *Roundabout* rounded first with several boats right behind her. Then the wind dropped completely, allowing those behind to carry the wind to the mark, thus closing up the fleet for a new race to the finish. The Sound is without tide, and consequently one would think without current, but there is the unmeasurable phenomenon called "drift." It affects a boat in the same way as tide. This drift is caused by the friction of the wind over the water surface. Thus, as we sat becalmed off this mark, trying to beat south, we actually drifted north, backward and away from the finish. Almost everyone anchored upon reaching the mark.

These conditions didn't last long. Soon a light southerly came in which saw anchors up and light sails being tended with constant care. Following the light southerly was a big black cloud moving across the water toward us. We made a quick change to the #2 genoa and were almost ready for it when it hit us. Neither we nor anyone else was ready for what we got. The wind increased from 10 knots to over 30 knots in an instant, knocking the fleet over on its ear. We heeled over so that water was spilling over the leeward rail into the cockpit. I dove to release the genoa sheet and someone else did the same on the main sheet. We righted quickly. Stunned by the force of the impact, and wondering how long it would last, we lay with sails a quarter filled. It was obvious that the conditions were here to stay. We had to get some sail down and get going. This wasn't going to be a momentary blast that would leave us in calm again. It would take too much time to change the headsail, so the main was dropped completely. We were probably the first to get under way again with some manner of orderliness. Many boats tried to carry on under full sail. None of them were happy doing it. Just as we settled down, sailing past several boats still completely overpowered, someone on the foredeck yelled something about the spinnaker pole. I was still to leeward, having just cleated the genoa sheet, and saw it floating past some 2 feet away from our lee rail. Somehow I lunged over the lifelines and grabbed the pole before it got by. I ended up bent over the lifelines with head and shoulders underwater and the pole in one outstretched hand. With a few additional hands both the pole and I returned to the boat only a little damper than before—if that was at all possible, for the cloud had brought sheets of driving rain.

It was awe-inspiring to watch the reactions of the boats as they were hit by the blast of wind, and to see how quickly they recovered and took up the race again. The wind finally eased. We reset the main for a closely fought beat to the finish line. *Roundabout* maintained her position and finished first, some 2½ minutes ahead of "The Blue Dane"—*Jettebeth IV*. Then came *Robin,* and *Yeoman* beat us across the line after a close tacking duel as we neared the finish.

That blast of wind nearly spelled disaster for us. Had the spinnaker pole gotten away we would have had big problems, for it was the only one we had. It would have been nearly impossible to find a re-

Tina's bendy mast after the Ocean Race

placement before the start of the ocean race the following day. Far more serious was a bend which developed two-thirds of the way up the mast as a result of the squall.

It wasn't going to be easy to straighten the spar, especially with time a major factor. Who could tell how much damage had been done, or how much punishment the mast could now take?

We had our work cut out for us that evening. By the time we arrived at a plan of attack most places of business were closed, but with the assistance of the Yacht Club we found a rigger who would work on the problem that evening. It was well after dark when he started securing a new set of intermediate upper stays. They were fastened to the mast halfway between the top and the spreaders. The other end was secured to the outer end of the spreaders, thus giving the necessary support to the upper half of the mast to eliminate the bend that had developed.

We couldn't do much to help, so retired to our bunks as he worked on under floodlights. Some time after midnight he finished.

In the morning we powered back to the basin for breakfast with our fingers crossed. Our attempts to conceal our troubles were in vain, for with our absence that night and our need for assistance word of our problem got around quickly. Out of curiosity about our bendy spar, a great many eyes closely inspected us as we returned to our berth.

It was a hectic morning preparing for the ocean race. The start was at 1:00 P.M. off Helsingoer, 10 miles to the north. We followed the procession powering north, busily stowing food and gear.

The wind was light for the start and beginning to change. This was no ordinary ocean race. It was fought and sailed like a regular around-the-buoy day race sailed in one-design boats. The start set the atmosphere. All 24 boats were across within 10 seconds of each other.

The wind increased continuously throughout the evening. We worked into the leading group almost immediately, with *Roundabout, Diana, Clarionet,* and *Goodwin* well spotted as darkness fell. Our spar problem seemed to be all right, or at least on the port tack the mast stood nearly straight. Around seven o'clock we tacked onto the starboard tack and our hearts began to sink. There was the same bend that had developed the day before. The new intermediate upper had weight on it, for it was much straighter than we had been able to get it by hand. Would it hold? What could we do? There was no answer to the first question and nothing we could do to help it. We continued on, hoping that it would stay up.

I recall the 8-to-12 watch very well. The wind increased in strength, with the seas building up short and steep. We changed to the #2 genoa and then decided it was time to reef the main. With John Carter steering, Don Pye and I tackled the reefing job. Considering the conditions—a sloping, bouncing wet deck and nearly total darkness—we accomplished the task in good form. Or at least Don and I thought so. John, sitting in the peaceful cockpit, wasn't so sure. He didn't let us rest long before wanting the main halyard pulled up tighter; the luff was much too loose.

Don and I went forward again. With both of us on the main halyard winch handle, he pulling and I pushing, we got a few more

Kattegat

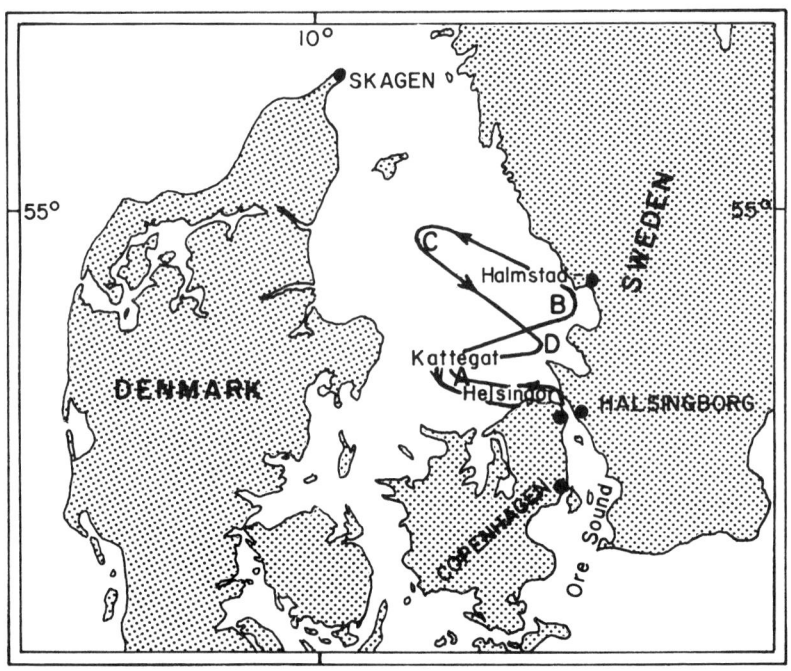

A. KATTEGAT S.W. L.V.
B. SKORREN BUOY
C. AALBORG BUGT L.V.
D. KATTEGAT S. L.V.

clicks on the winch. It still wasn't enough. So we put our strength to it once again. Bang! The mainsail came sliding down and part of the winch brake mechanism hit the deck once before falling overboard.

It is hard to roll in a good reef without equal pressure along the whole sail. This is most easily performed when the sail is up and can be lowered as the reef is rolled in. But trying to roll in several turns with the sail on deck is hard enough even under good conditions. We had far from that, and near darkness to boot. The topping lift had been removed prior to the race's start to eliminate some unnecessary wind resistance. With the main down this left the boom free-wheeling around the deck.

We finally got the main back up; the winch worked all right as long as we left the handle in and held it. So that's what we did, lashing it to the mast. This gave us a poor-looking reefing job, but at least we had the main back up, and the mast was still standing.

Time passed and the wind increased some more. Once again we were exceeding the desired angle of heel. Theoretically it is no problem to roll in another few rolls to compensate for the increased heel, but, with our added trouble with the main halyard winch, that theoretically easy task changed from a one-man job to a battle. It had to be done again. Combining balance and brawn, Don and I managed two more rolls without major mishap.

The sail was so poorly reefed by now that it was doing next to no good. We conferred, in the relatively dry cockpit, and decided to replace the poorly reefed main with the storm trysail. It was finally pulled from the bag (stowed in the extreme forward part of the forepeak) and set. We convinced ourselves that the load on the bending mast was safer now and that we were making better time than before. But after an hour under this ridiculous rig we pulled ourselves together and got the main decently reefed and reset.

Dick has a vivid memory of that 4-hour watch as well. Not a wink did he sleep, though he was stretched out in a dry comfortable bunk. On each wave, which seemed to be a little bigger or a little steeper than the last, he expected to hear the mast go over the side. There seemed to be no reason why it didn't. We were doing considerable pounding, and the wind reached 40 knots. Still it stood.

During our watch we had lost track of our competitors. We weren't optimistic about our position as we approached the first mark. Our shenanigans with the main certainly must have cost us positions. In addition, the bend in the mast caused the forestay to sag way off, making the boat anything but a windward machine.

Much to our surprise, we could see only two lights just ahead of us. Were we third around after all? The personnel on the light vessel confirmed this; *Diana* and *Clarionet* were the only ones ahead of us.

The next mark, some 40 miles away off the Swedish coast, was nearly a broad reach. Up went the spinnaker and down we went in two consecutive broaches. With disappointment on one hand and relief on the other, we took the spinnaker off. Although we were back on the port tack we had no idea what the condition of the spar was. *Roundabout,* in fifth position, held well below the course and was probably carrying her spinnaker. Later on the wind eased and we reset the kite without the earlier difficulties.

Although *Tina* carried a penalty on the size of her spinnaker we couldn't overtake the two ahead of us as quickly as we had hoped. We never did catch *Clarionet* on that leg; she rounded the Skorren mark 5 minutes ahead of us in a light breeze that had left the seas extra large for the wind's strength. This is where *Tina* really turned on. Hard on the wind, with the big genoa slightly eased, the trim tab set for windward lift, and Dick at the helm, we not only sailed past *Clarionet* but passed her to windward. This completely demoralized them, as it would have us or anyone else in a similar situation. They changed sail trim and helmsmen two or three times in an attempt to hang on to us. Nothing worked. *Tina* opened up our lead to 50 minutes at the next mark.

Tina had a fantastically easy motion through waves. People had commented about this earlier, but not until now did we realize that it was due to *Tina*'s wineglass-shaped hull. The conditions here, a light breeze, much lighter than the seas indicated, were ideal for her. *Clarionet* and the rest of the fleet just didn't have the same motion through waves as *Tina* did. They hobby-horsed along, stopped by every other wave, while we rode the chop easily. It is a frustrating position to be in, but all the more so when another boat isn't affected by the chop and sails on by.

For the rest of the race the gap between *Tina* and *Clarionet* was never less than 30 minutes. We finished as the sun was rising early Monday morning, very happy, very tired, and thankful not to be back a few positions where there was still a hard-fought contest. *Clarionet* was also unchallenged. But *Roundabout* had bloodhounds gnawing at her heels constantly. At Aalborg Buoy she was 16 minutes ahead of *Ian XIV* (Sweden). But on the 60-mile run to the Kattegat South Light Vessel, *Roundabout* saw her rivals close in on her. In particular, *Aladdin,* almost the smallest boat in the fleet, climbed into fourth place, 2 minutes behind her. The threatening downwind flying hull of *Robin* was only 3 minutes farther astern. They weren't the only ones. Between the third and eleventh boats, after 48 hours and over 200 miles of racing, there was only half an hour's difference.

Late Sunday evening, after rounding the last mark with 35 miles to the finish, *Roundabout* was still clinging to third place. If she could hang on she would, on aggregate, be only one point behind *Tina*. But the wind gods were not with her. Almost immediately *Robin* reached by, followed shortly by *Aladdin.*

During the night the wind changed, providing for a beat to the finish in dead light airs. Some chose the shore, others went offshore. Van de Stadt, revelling in the light conditions, nursed *Aladdin* across the finish line third, followed by *De Schelde, Robin, Jettebeth, Ian XIV,* and *Roundabout*. At the finish, between the third and tenth boats, after 60 hours of racing, there were only 44 minutes. This was real round-the-buoy racing.

The next day, a rest day, was spent doing just that. That "ocean race" was the longest day race I have ever been on. Even though we stood regular watches, the constant navigational problems and sailing required continual assistance from the off watch. As it happened we divided up, with Sammy Sampson as navigator on Dick's watch and Don Pye as back-up or check navigator on John's watch. This way

Tina's crew: (top) Don Pye, John Carter, Sam Sampson, (bottom) Sandy Weld, Edward Stettinius, Dick Carter. The beach ball Dick is holding nearly sailed past us during a calm period of the Ocean Race.

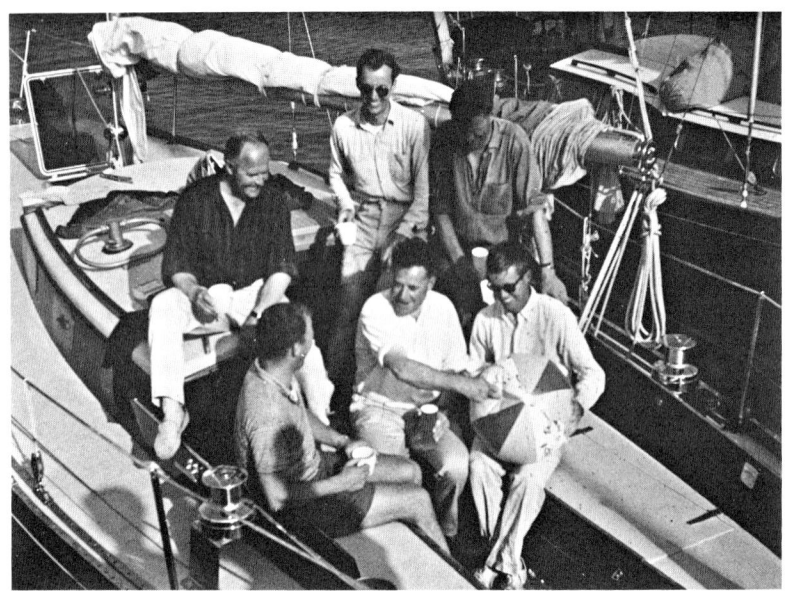

we kept constant track of our location and of that of the next buoy. This would have been almost an impossible task for one person, due to the length of the course and the large number of turning marks. It was a tremendous help for us, with both men complementing each other extremely well.

One task that we undertook at our leisure during rest day was to rerig the intermediate uppers. We now had a permanent "S" in the upper portion of the mast. The spar's experimental inner supports were the only reason it remained standing. The apparent problem lay in a flaw in one section of the spar. But it had to last for another race. After the first night out on the ocean race both of the new port and starboard intermediate uppers had been as loose as wet spaghetti. The idea was fine, but the rigger had not been able to attach the intermediate stays to the main shroud tightly enough to prevent them from riding up the wire. To have attached the intermediate stays to the end of the spreaders would only have weakened them as well. This time we accepted the additional windage of another wire running down from the spreaders and brought the intermediate uppers right down to the deck. This would have to hold the mast straight, we hoped.

The press calculated for us that if we came in at least eighth in the last race we would win the whole series. That was nice of them, but no one on board *Tina* had the slightest thought of relaxing and trying for a nice safe eighth. We entered the last race as keyed up as though it were the first. We had one thought: to win this race.

There are three areas of the race that I remember particularly well. The first one was at the start. There was practically no wind all morning. A few minutes before the starting gun it swung around into the northeast so that one could hardly fetch the line on the starboard tack, the tack everyone had previously selected. After the gun almost everyone stood off to the north on the starboard tack.

We too started on the starboard, and found ourselves in a not very favorable position due to the wind change. We had to get away from the fleet, if for no other reason than to get clear wind. Seeing the two Danes, *Diana* and *Jettebeth,* head off on the port tack to the east made us tack post haste. In such conditions, local knowledge is extremely important, and to let two such boats go off unheaded would be pure folly. Besides, for what it was worth, the morning forecast was for easterlies.

Robin followed us to the east; the remainder of the fleet stood to the north. With the fleet split, it was a sure sign of disaster for one group and joy for the other. Then the calm came, and for 15 minutes most boats lost steerageway completely, slatting and flogging fretfully. Conditions were worse to the north than in our group. Then the new easterly came, slowly at first, but with a deliberation that hinted at its serious purpose. *Diana* was first to feel it, then, one by one, the rest of us that had stood to the east. Suddenly we were 2 miles dead to windward of the other group. The wind was soon blowing 15 knots. The die was cast. Or was it? Would the wind veer south of east so that those to leeward might lay the mark? The wind held steady, and even those of us to the east had a short hitch to make the mark.

Diana led us around by a couple of minutes. We sneaked around in front of *Robin* and then reached for a mark to the south. *Diana* held high, hoping to be able to set her spinnaker. *Tina* and *Robin* ran the rhumb line. We rounded first with *Robin* close behind. The ensuing run was uneventful except for setting the stage for the second sequence of events that I recall so vividly.

Coming into the leeward mark we were leading, with *Robin* close on our windward quarter. Somehow—I was too busy to see how—*Robin* rounded the mark ahead of us. We in fact made a near-perfect rounding, with the buoy close aboard as we cranked the genoa in the last few inches and *Tina* carried her momentum through the rounding. *Robin,* having approached closer to the buoy when rounding, had to take a wider course on the leeward side of the buoy. She lost some of her speed due to the tightness of the rounding. It was nip and tuck as to whether we would ride over *Robin* or not. We did, and then we just pounded to windward and ahead of *Robin* on the beat to windward in a steadily increasing wind.

As we approached the windward mark, the wind picked up to 25 to 30 knots. We had been using the #2 genoa the whole leg and were now carrying too much sail. But with the short distance left to go it was less time-consuming to lug it than to shorten sail.

As we rounded, the spinnaker was up, set flying as always. It was blowing so hard that it took an incredible amount of effort to winch the halyard up. The head of the sail was some 4 feet from the top of the mast when it filled, and I didn't dare winch it up any further. It felt as though the halyard were jammed aloft. As we drove toward our next mark, about half a mile from the finish, we discussed the problem with some concern. Finally, by hoisting the genoa again, which took much of the wind away from the spinnaker, I was able to hoist it the remainder of the way without difficulty.

With things back to nearly normal, I took stock of the surroundings. It was then that I realized that, barring a complete disaster—such as the mast finally going over the side—we were not only going to win the One Ton Cup but also this race. *Robin,* having just rounded the mark, didn't hoist her spinnaker in any hurry. We were sailing through the rest of the fleet, still on the way to the weather mark. That was the greatest moment of the whole series.

I don't know if anyone on board thought about not putting the spinnaker up immediately upon rounding the windward mark. I certainly didn't and don't believe anyone else did either. The maneuver was as simple as rolling off a log; the next leg was nearly a dead run and there is never a question as to whether one carries a spinnaker or not.

Disaster didn't strike, and we went on to win the race and series. If it had, someone was bound to have said we shouldn't have set the spinnaker; we had a substantial lead on the second place boat, not to mention the eighth place boat, and were practically assured of winning the series. The fact that this was not mentioned by anyone, if even thought of by anyone on board, was far more gratifying than crossing the finish line first.

The question asked again and again was where the series would be held next year. Not in Annapolis, U.S.A., as far as the Europeans were concerned. It would be sure ruin for the series, they felt; no one could afford to participate. But conversely would it not make it easier for a Canadian or Argentinian entry or two, thus widening the scope of and interest in the series? Certainly the wherewithal is available in each country represented in the Copenhagen series to field a top-notch team of three boats for a series in the United States.

The question wasn't answered then, nor indeed until several months later. It was decided, in the best interest of the series, to hold it in European waters. The location selected was Le Havre, France.

"In the best interest of the series" raises many questions. What is in the best interest of the One Ton series? Where is this series headed? What is its future?

The concept of racing boats of different design on an equal basis had an enthusiastic and spontaneous beginning. Following the first One Ton series the "Half Ton" was formulated by the La Rochelle Yacht Club, and Italy immediately began plans for a similar series in larger boats, which was quickly dubbed the "Two Ton Cup."

The tremendous increase in competition between the first and second series was staggering. But is it really so surprising? Competitive pressure is constantly increasing throughout the world of sports. Why not in ocean racing as well? The first sign of it was in 1965 when England produced three new boats with the expressed intent of defending the Admiral's Cup. The nostalgic appeal of racing boat-for-boat was quickly reappraised by the One Ton Cup series with the realization that this type of racing under ocean racing's environment placed even greater pressure on designers, builders, and crew.

Times haven't changed much; boats have, as well as the equipment and crews, but the principle of competition hasn't. In 1936 Alfred Loomis wrote about the double staysail schooner *Nina*'s 1928 Fastnet win: "She won boat for boat and easily saved her time. So *Nina* brought home to her critics the fact that when an ocean-racing prize is worth defending it must be defended with modern boats that are sea going as well as sea keeping." This is exactly what is taking place today, but at a much higher level, in series such as the Admiral's Cup in England, the S.O.R.C. in the U.S., and most particularly the One Ton Cup. If it is worth trying to win it is worth attacking with the best boats available.

There are opponents to the One Ton rules. Some want to take it out from the R.O.R.C. measurement rule. Some claim that a change in the R.O.R.C. rule could well change a One Ton boat's rating so that it would no longer be practical to compete. Others want to change the rule to eliminate discrepancies arising from this or that type of boat. Still others want more races, particularly day races. The One Ton Cup could become one of the great yachting events in the world. The I.Y.R.A. has given serious consideration to it as a future Olympic class. Whatever the future brings, I hope the emphasis is placed on offshore racing rather than day races. It is the offshore racing that will ensure development of healthy ocean racing boats rather than stripped-out around-the-buoy racing machines.

I was amazed at the reports of the English press on the One Ton series. Invariably they credited *Tina*'s win to Dick's fine sailing (a point I certainly don't dispute), but maintained that boat for boat both *Roundabout* and *Clarionet* were better designed. Jack Knights reported: "The way I see it *Tina*'s win was through good sailing rather than design. She is not the equal of *Roundabout* in a hard breeze upwind and it is doubtful whether she could hold *Roundabout* upwind in lightish airs provided the sea was moderate. However, there's no doubt that she is a flyer off the wind."

The performances of the three boats indicated nearly the opposite to me. *Tina*'s ability to get to windward (not necessarily her ability to point closer to the wind) in any kind of conditions, as well as her reaching performance, was better than either *Roundabout*'s or *Clarionet*'s. However, *Tina*'s running speed was only equal to or possibly slightly better than that of the two British boats. Is it so hard to believe that *Rabbit*'s and *Tina*'s successes were at least partly due to good design?

Rabbit II *sailing through* Fanfare's *lee on the Solent*

11. *Rabbit II*

IN 1967 I was back in Cowes looking for *Rabbit II,* Dick's latest design and member of the U.S. Admiral's Cup team. Our teammates were *Thunderbird,* T.V. Learson's 1966 Bermuda Race winning Cal 40, and *Figaro IV,* Bill Snaith's internationally known S.O.R.C. winner. Potentially we were a strong team. *Figaro IV* had removed her mizzen and shortened the foot of her mainsail in an effort to reduce her R.O.R.C. rating. *Thunderbird* had on board a battery of top-notch sailors such as Lowell North, Bob Symonnette, and Bill Lapworth. All we needed now was some results.

It wasn't going to be easy: that was obvious. *Thunderbird's* rating was so outlandishly high she would be sailing in Class I. For comparison, *Rabbit II* is two feet longer and rates close to the bottom of Class II. We were going to have to learn about and tune *Rabbit II* during the series. There had been little time for such activity before the series.

The English team had been selected after 7 elimination races were held for the many interested boats. The top boat was Dennis Miller's *Firebrand,* with a separate rudder and skeg added for this season. The largest was Ron Amey's brand-new *Noryema V,* built to the design of Peter Nicholson. The third British boat, Arthur Slater's *Prospect of Whitby,* is of Stephens design, slightly earlier but of the same size and design as *Firebrand.*

The Australian team consisted of Bob Creighton-Brown's *Balandra; Caprice of Huon,* sailed this year by Gordon Reynolds with practically the same crew that was on board in 1965; and a new boat, *Mercedes III,* designed and owned by Ted Kaufman. What marked them right from the start was their determination to win.

Six other countries were represented in this year's Admiral's Cup, with a total of 26 competitors. The competition has been increasing steadily since 1957, when several Englishmen proposed such a series, at that time called the British Challenge Cup. The deed of gift establishes the contest biennially in Fastnet years, with competition by teams of three boats from each country. The Cup is to be sailed for in two day races sandwiched in between two long distance races: the

Channel Race and Fastnet. In 1957 the British team of *Uomie, Myth of Malham,* and *Jocasta* beat an American team of *Carina* (who won the Fastnet Race), *Figaro,* and *White Mist* by 3 points. In 1959 the British won, a little more easily, against teams from Holland and France. 1961 saw the Cup spend some time in New York when it was won by an American team consisting of *Cyane* (Henry B. duPont), *Figaro* (Bill Snaith), and *Windrose* (Jakob Isbrandtsen). The English won the Cup back in 1963 against an ever-increasing field. In 1965 they held on, although formidably challenged by seven countries led by the tough, well-organized Australians.

For generations Cowes Week has been the peak of the European, if not the world, yachting season. This is still true, but the emphasis at Cowes has changed. If any one event has encouraged this change, it is the Admiral's Cup competition, which has perhaps reached the status of ocean racing's top international sporting event.

The Channel Race started off Portsmouth in a light southwesterly that soon freshened to 15 to 20 knots. Genoas were carried to Horse Sand Fort, then spinnakers were set for the broad reach to the Owers and the run up Channel to the Royal Sovereign. Sunset provided a beautiful sight of multi-colored spinnakers reaching out to the Owers.

Eric Tabarly's single-handed transatlantic sensation, *Pen Duick III,* rounded the Royal Sovereign first, followed by the new German *Rubin.* In Class II *Mercedes* led *Firebrand* and us on the broad reach across Channel to the Le Havre buoy. *Mercedes* and *Caprice* rounded before the wind dropped and the tide turned against us. We battled with *Firebrand,* trying to reach the buoy against a fading wind and increasing tide. The buoy stayed a tantalizing quarter mile to weather for several hours. Several times during our struggles both boats were within 100 yards of each other and were hard on the wind heading directly at each other. Finally the tide began to gain the upper hand, forcing us to anchor for an hour with *Firebrand* anchored right beside us. It was frustrating to think of the Australians with the tide under their sterns heading for the finish.

Firebrand *on the Solent*
Mercedes *III* (Below)

[135]

Caprice of Huon

When the southwest wind freshened, up to 20 knots, it filled in first out in the Channel, widening the gap between the leaders and the rest of the fleet. *Pen Duick* led the fleet all the way, finishing first and saving her time on everyone. For the Admiral's Cup boats, *Rubin* (Germany) placed second, then *Mercedes* (Australia), *Balandra* (Australia), *Rabbit II* (U.S.), *Noryema V* (England), *Caprice* (Australia), and *Firebrand* (England).

The Australians were off to a rapid start with a 3, 4, and 7. The English, standing in second, had finishes of 6, 8, and 13. *Rabbit*'s 5th was badly offset by *Figaro*'s 24th. She had snagged a lobster pot Friday evening off the Owers, which wasn't discovered until the next morning. *Thunderbird*'s tenth rounded out our team's total points, placing the U.S. in fifth. The English weren't overly concerned, and there were still ample points left for the U.S. team to come through.

The first of the two inshore races is the Britannia Cup, which is part of Cowes Week proper as well as being an Admiral's Cup event. There were 60-odd entries, of which 26 were Admiral's Cup boats. A

The clipper-bowed schooner Pen Duick III

moderate southwesterly gave a long beat to the first mark off Hampstead Ledge. *Pen Duick* led the fleet around, followed by the 90-foot *Gitana* and half a dozen top Class I and II boats. We were delighted to be in the group, and pleased that we had boat speed to windward on our larger foes. We held in close to the Island shore for the run to the northeast Ryde Middle. We were too close at one moment and smacked onto a rock, a known but unmarked hazard to those hugging the shore. Luckily it was only a momentary stop.

The second time around found the wind lightening and a real boat-for-boat battle developed between *Firebrand, Mercedes, Noryema, Caprice,* and *Rabbit II. Pen Duick* kept her lead over *Gitana*, who had to stay well out in the strong tide. We crossed the line third followed by *Firebrand, Mercedes, Noryema, Oryx, Rubin, Caprice,* and *Balandra*.

It wasn't until after the race that the storm hit. Several of the Dutch boats had stopped after the first round, after misreading a confusing shortened course signal. The Race Committee disqualified others for passing the wrong side of the offshore starting line marker at the end of the first round. Still others were disqualified for crossing through the starting line on the run down to the Ryde Middle buoy when it should have been avoided. *Oryx* protested us for doing this. At the protest hearing neither party showed up (we hadn't heard about it), so the protest lapsed. By the afternoon of the next day *Oryx* had the matter reopened. This time her protest was dismissed since she had flown no protest flag. The Race Committee was in the awkward position of not having seen us, but of suspecting that we had not conformed exactly with the course as described in the race circular.

To find in the race circular the infringement we were alleged to have made, we looked in the back of the circular under a section called "Postponements." This seemed an extremely odd place to find course instructions. We were indeed in error; we had passed the offshore mark to port rather than to starboard. Not having been concerned with postponements, we were not aware that this marker was part of our course at this point in the race, and since the mark (described in the circular as a buoy) was actually a large motor vessel it was deemed better seamanship on our part to leave it to windward,

Rabbit II *battling with the Class I* Norvema V

thus to port, than to leeward. It made absolutely no difference to us, nor did it affect our position in the slightest. But that was beside the point; we had disobeyed the course instructions.

Wednesday, Dick withdrew his declaration, disqualifying himself from the race, which *Rabbit II* had otherwise won. Interestingly enough, in the 1969 race circular these particular instructions were no longer to be found under the heading of "Postponements."

We were not the only Admiral's Cup boat to lose out on disqualification. *Pen Duick* and six others were rubbed from the final results.

Our withdrawal left *Mercedes* the winner of the Britannia Cup and dealt a further serious blow to American chances. Australia increased her lead over the British by only one point, to 27. The big change was for Finland's team, up two places into fourth. We made room for them by dropping into sixth.

The next race, the New York Yacht Club Challenge Cup, produced some of the most varied and exciting conditions possible. The race started in a moderate southwesterly, and the start was quickly

Figaro *with her R.O.R.C. racing rig*

followed by one of several heavy rain squalls. *Rabbit II* thrived in the heavy going as we kept busy on board while the squalls passed overhead. *Gitana* revelled in the conditions, in which she was just able to carry full sail. She was a beautiful sight as she steadily increased her lead throughout the day, finishing 40 minutes ahead of the next boat—quite a lead in a 33-mile race. The course consisted of a fairly small triangle to the west of Cowes and then a long run before beating back to the finish. The bottom leg of the triangle produced some exciting reaching, under shy spinnakers and 20 knots of wind.

The next run was a busy one on board most of the boats. The course was dead before an increasing sou'wester. The black clouds had disappeared, and had been replaced by scattered white cumulus clouds and bright blue sky. The water turned into the dark green that is the unusual characteristic of the Solent. The sun sparkled off the shimmering water, making it a fantastic day for photographers. Unfortunately on *Rabbit II* we hardly had time to appreciate the beauty.

Upon rounding the windward mark for the long run, the regular spinnaker was set in quick time. Before we were able to get the genoa down and the foredeck in some semblance of order, *Rabbit II* started to yaw considerably. With the wind dead astern and the seas off one quarter it made steering downright difficult. Almost everyone tacked downwind to reduce the danger of a flying gybe, and—so the helmsman said—to get out of the slowly building head tide.

We had the spinnaker rigged with double guy and sheet, with the opening on the outboard end of the spinnaker pole up for a dip-the-pole gybe. Because of the continued yawing, the movement of the wire guy worked the spinnaker pole pin open, letting the spinnaker fly free. It was fortunate that we had the double guy and sheet, but it was no easy task to resecure the guy to the outboard end of the pole. The wind pressure on the spinnaker was tremendous, and of course the spinnaker was well above one's reach. With Jon Wales (the spinnaker expert on the American 12-meter *Nefertiti*) in the cockpit handling the double guy, I was able to gain control of the spinnaker again.

Unfortunately, this happened three or four times, and we gybed three times—intentionally, but not using the dippy pole method. Things were too wild for that. We used two poles. Jon's competence in the cockpit made easy work of it for those of us on the foredeck. It all happened in a matter of 10 miles, at a speed of 9 to 10 knots. I had time for only quick glances at the wild antics of the fleet.

Through our own antics our spinnaker developed a small tear. Quickly we prepared the reaching spinnaker, a much flatter sail, and carefully and quickly lowered the one with the tear. With the reaching spinnaker up and the spinnaker pole's opening turned down we had less trouble, yawing less and not flipping the guy out of the pole.

The final beat back past Castle Point was exhausting. Many of the local boats stayed well off the point, knowing that to get too close to Castle Point was fatal. The risk of being blanketed was almost a certainty. We stayed in close, tacking frequently, and picked up on those who "knew better."

The final stretch up through the anchored fleet was near agony. But our tacking efficiency didn't slacken, for the excitement was overpowering. All the top boats were there as well and we were racing them on a boat-for-boat basis to the line. On corrected time it looked close between *Firebrand, Mercedes,* and us for first place.

All that spinnaker trouble and the tiring last beat were made all the more worthwhile, for we did win. *Firebrand* was second, followed by the consistent three Australians. When the Admiral's Cup points were brought up to date it could be seen immediately that the cards were between Australia (285 points) and England (241 points). Then came Germany (199) and the U.S. (175). Even though the Fastnet points count treble (as against the Channel Race double points and each of the day races single points), the Australian lead of 44 points would be hard to crack, barring unforeseen disaster. The Australian approach was simply more professional, more dedicated, more cohesive, and better organized than that of the other countries. In the three completed races all three Australian boats were in the top seven each time, a measure of consistency that doesn't leave much room for anyone else.

In talking with Graham Newland, off *Caprice,* and other Australians Thursday evening, I learned that they were much impressed with *Rabbit II*'s performance. But it really galled them, so they said, for us to win, in essence, both day races while acting as a ferry. (During both races Polly Carter and her 8-year-old daughter had joined our escapades over the Solent.) "Here we are," said Graham, "hard on the wind, everyone amidships and flat on the windward rail. There you are, beating us in a smaller boat with Polly and daughter enjoying themselves in the stern!"

Fastnet Eve was quiet, with nothing vicious in the forecast. Indeed, there was practically a flat calm as the 150 boats from 12 countries made their way out to the start. Class I started at 9:45 with ghosters and light sheets rigged. The gentle westerly brought up the age-old problem of whether to start in the eddy along Cowes Green or at the outer limit mark and head straight for the mainland shore. There was still a good hour of flood tide to contend with. Class I split on this decision and *Pen Duick, Thunderbird, Noryema, Kittywake,* and, of all boats, *Gitana,* went for the Island shore. *Gitana,* with her deep draft and 90-foot length, found rock-dodging off Egypt Point not really her type of sailing and was the first to strike out into the Solent.

Class II also split, and we found ourselves trading tacks with *Mercedes, Caprice,* and *Firebrand* close in along the Cowes shore.

The Italian *Levantades,* who led Class I to the mainland shore, was the first through the Needles Channel. Once we were clear of the Solent the westerly filled in, giving a good beat down the Channel with several hours of ebb still left. Most stood straight out into the Channel on a long starboard tack. We were still battling with *Mercedes, Caprice,* and *Firebrand* as we began to pick off part of Class I. Just before dark the trio we were fighting with tacked onto the port tack. Not wanting to let them get away, we followed. Then during the darkness with lights coming and going we lost them. They obviously had returned to the starboard tack. We held on into West Bay, behind Start Point, spending the early morning hours in light winds. Those that took the long starboard tack were able to tack and ease sheets Sunday as the wind backed into the south, enabling them to clear the Lizard. As we were in under the shore the Lizard was still a beat for us.

Once we were past the Lizard Sunday afternoon the wind began to strengthen, still from the south with swells rolling in from the southwest. Off the Seven Stones, near midnight, we were bowling along on a broad reach in pitch darkness and force 6 to 7 winds. Steering was wild in the awkward cross seas, reminiscent of two years before. *Rabbit II* rode the seas well, although often two people were required on the tiller, one pulling, the other pushing.

During the early morning darkness the spinnaker halyard frayed through, dropping the spinnaker head into the water to leeward. We pulled it back aboard without its entwining anything underwater, even though we had sailed over most of it and had to pull it in over the stern. Under the genoa we continued on, maintaining nearly the same speed.

As the wind died in the early morning hours, the spinnaker was rehoisted on the genoa halyard. With daylight Dick was hoisted to the top of the mast to replace the spinnaker halyard.

Gitana rounded the Rock at 0600 Monday, 7 hours ahead of her record-breaking passage in 1965. Second was *Pen Duick,* which had obviously enjoyed the hard downwind sail. She turned at 1025. Then came *Rubin* at 1110, *Figaro* at 1122, *Carina* (U.S.) at 1158, and the rest of the fleet. The first boat in Class II to round was *Caprice* at 1604, followed by teammate *Mercedes* at 1650. We were well back, running in to the Rock in a dying wind. We rounded in sloppy seas and started the long beat back, for what wind there was had backed further into the southeast.

Since leaving the Lizard Sunday afternoon we had seen hardly another boat. Where were they? Could a majority of the fleet be behind us? Or was it all ahead of us? Even when bearing down on the Rock we had been alone. On the beat back we stood to the south, finding one calm area after another. All day Tuesday we chased clouds, hoping to find a little more wind under them. Most of the time we were not successful. Wednesday morning the breeze strengthened and swung back into the south, enabling us to ease

Rabbit II, *with Dick Carter at the helm, rounding* Fastnet Rock

sheets and finally set spinnaker. Off the Bishop Rock boats were in sight, but at too great a distance to be recognized. Where was everyone?

Off the Lizard we spotted *Tina*. It was some relief to learn that she had withdrawn from the race after breaking a spreader. Wednesday evening we reached slowly toward Plymouth, still wondering where the fleet was. Had they all finished?

As we approached abeam of the Eddystone Light, 16 miles off Plymouth, the wind petered out. It took us six hours to cover the next 16 miles, finally getting a morning breeze inside the entrance for the short distance to the finish. We crossed the line mid-morning Thursday.

Gitana wasn't able to break her own record. As she neared the Scilly Isles in strong head winds (while we were becalmed) she started having trouble. First her jib halyard went, then the mainsail headboard pulled out. With the wind at 30 knots and a matching sea there was no question of anybody trying to climb to the peak of her 120-foot mast. They jury-rigged halyards for greatly reduced sail and limped on.

Pen Duick had finished first at 0139 Wednesday, with *Figaro* next in at 0623. Then came *Outlaw* (England), *Carina* (by now a two-time Fastnet winner), *Levantades, Rubin,* and *Oryx*. *Mercedes* was first in Class II at 1608 Wednesday, followed by *Caprice* and two hours later by *Firebrand*.

On corrected time *Pen Duick* again saved her time on the fleet. *Figaro* recouped her Channel Race miseries with a second overall. We ended up 19th, having fallen behind the first night out and never having been able to get back into the wind pattern that carried the leaders on around the course.

The Australian team came in with another top performance, placing 3, 4, and 7, pushing their total points to 495; 107 points more than the second place British team. The U.S. group compiled 183 points during the Fastnet, which moved us into third, ahead of France and Germany.

During the prize-giving ceremonies, Ron Amey, captain of the

British Admiral's Cup team, described the winners as *"Mercedes,* a home-built something-or-other. *Balandra,* a design four years behind the times. *Caprice,* a 16-year-old lump of wood." He was being purposely hypercritical of these boats to emphasize what was the near unanimous opinion concerning Australia's quite extraordinary success—their crews were so much better as a team than any of the others.

Mercedes was the high individual scorer with one win and three thirds, a truly fine performance and a credit to Ted Kaufman and his top-notch crew.

The boat that attracted the most attention was Eric Tabarly's new *Pen Duick.* Her rig is the most imaginative: she is schooner rigged, with the two alloy spars almost the same length. Between these she sets either a fully battened foresail or a huge overlapping fisherman staysail or "golliwobbler" with a wishbone gaff sheeted to the mainmast head. With spinnaker, golliwobbler, main, and genoa up she boasts about 3,340 square feet of sail! *Pen Duick* is close-winded as no schooner ought to be. Downwind she is extremely fast, in light or heavy going. Even with a high rating of over 37 feet she was not only the first home, but winner on handicap in the Channel Race and Fastnet. This is all the more intriguing because she was built as a super solo transatlantic racer which has no regard for ratings, while her competitors of recent design are designed very much with a rating rule in mind.

The Australians taught us all a lesson. Who would put it into practice in 1969? The Australians would of course be back, determined to thwart any and all challengers. Would any country match their determination and supreme effort?

Red Rooster

12. *Red Rooster*

ON a Friday, July 11, 1969, I walked from the ferry landing in Breskens to Maas' Yard. There I was to meet Dick once again with his newest boat, *Red Rooster*. Sunday was scheduled for the first sail, so I was surprised not to see her floating at the dock. Instead, she was still inside the shed, with 20-odd men, nearly the whole yard, working on her. The program was to have a sail on Sunday, a few more days in the yard for last-minute work before sailing to Cowes for the Cowes-Dinard Race on July 18, and then to join the American Admiral's Cup team.

Had people thought that the previous Carter boats were all variations of the same design, there was no mistaking *Red Rooster* as something different. The most striking difference in *Rooster*'s design, and also the most controversial, was her centerboard, or more appropriately, swing keel. I'd heard Dick muse, as we were running in *Tina* or *Rabbit* or by the fireside, on what it would be like to round Fastnet Rock for the run back to Plymouth and be able to jettison the keel, or lift it completely into the hull. The first chance came when Ron Amey agreed to such a boat. Dick would design the boat (*Noryema VII*), leaving Ron, with his vast engineering background, to work out the mechanics of lifting (not jettisoning) some three tons of keel completely into the hull.

Wanting very much to learn from this experiment, Dick decided to build his own boat. Not having Ron's engineering and hydraulic knowledge to draw on, he decided to experiment with a more conventional mechanism, a swinging keel, on *Red Rooster*.

Red Rooster was a true centerboard boat, with no thought of a keel as there is on today's centerboard boats. The normal centerboard boat today is a combination keel and centerboard, with the centerboard, a heavy plate of steel, housed in the keel. This is a compromise between deep draft for going to windward and medium draft for running. Its advantage is that it is contained within the keel and does not interfere in the cabin. The disadvantage is that all the lifting mechanism is below water, difficult to get at and difficult to sophisticate. The real disadvantage of a normal centerboarder is

Rabbit II, Red Rooster

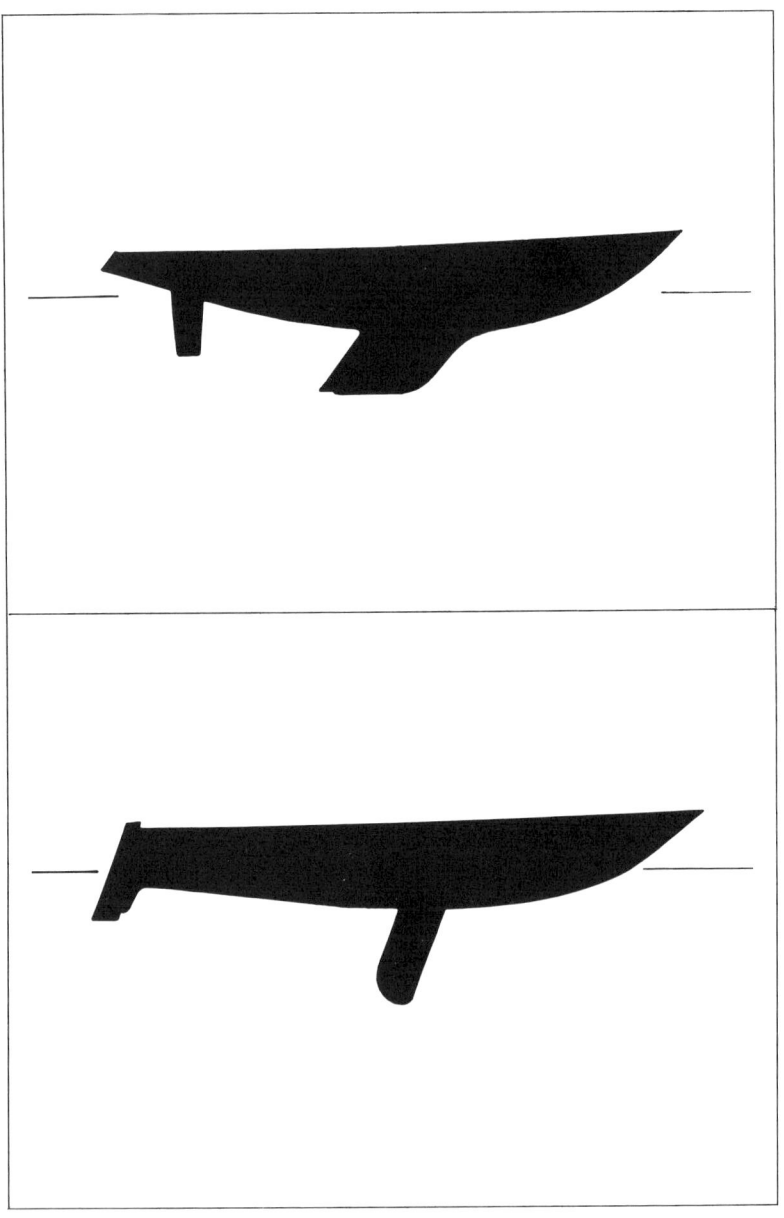

that it doesn't have the running capabilities that a centerboard boat should.

Red Rooster's hull had a draft of only 2 feet 9 inches with the swing keel up. On a 42-foot boat this is unusually little, but with the swing keel, nearly two tons of it, down, she drew 9 feet. *Red Rooster* was intended to conform to the true concept of centerboard boats.

The swing keel itself was a steel casing filled with lead. The shape of it was similar to those found on small centerboard boats, with very fine leading and trailing edges and a rounded end which is also bevelled. The keel swings on a huge pin supported by a large stainless steel brace, all an integral part of the centerboard box and hull.

A slot in the bottom of the hull some 7 feet long and 7 inches wide enabled the keel to enter the hull. With the keel up this slot would be a very large scoop, creating tremendous turbulence and drag. The same problem would arise with the keel lowered. Ingenuity produced a simple curtain of heavy rubber that could be pulled forward to seal the slot.

The rudder, with our new approach, hung off the stern and could be lifted almost out of the water. The theory behind this is the same as in motorboats: at high speeds you don't need a large surface to turn the boat. It is also at high speeds that steering becomes physically tiring with a big rudder, because of the large amount of water being pushed by the rudder. So, when running, if it is easier to steer with a smaller rudder, and just as, if not more, effective than the full-sized rudder, why not lift part of it out of the water?

Red Rooster's rig was similar to earlier Carter boats: large foretriangle with small mainsails. The mast was the same clean spar with internal roller reefing gear. The equipment on deck didn't change much, but for the first time Dick installed Brooks and Gatehouse wind speed and direction indicators. A simple novel device was created for the spinnaker sheet blocks on the transom. A cam lever turning block allowed sheets to be locked in position for rapid winch changes.

That evening work continued on *Red Rooster,* our enthusiasm picking up as the pieces began to fit together. Two days prior to my

Red Rooster. *Note rudder and hull configuration with swing keel up.*
Red Rooster *with swing keel down*

arrival the coach roof was not on and hardly any of the boat's interior had been completed. It was vitally important that we enter the Cowes-Dinard Race. A great deal was riding on *Red Rooster*'s success; she had been selected for the American Admiral's Cup team before being built, and (as far as we were concerned) would have to do well to justify her selection over a number of other interested American boats. With a phenomenon totally new to us, a swing keel, there were many things we had to learn. The best way to do this is in a race. And it had to be a race that wasn't part of the Admiral's Cup series so that we could experiment, something one doesn't normally do during a serious race.

Saturday evening *Red Rooster* was launched. There were two problems that confronted our sail Sunday. The engine wasn't hooked up, and the reduction gears for lifting the swing keel were too small. We could not physically lift the keel. It was important to sail Sunday with the keel in both positions, up and down. Since we launched with it up, there was no problem, except that to get out of the harbor we had to sail, a short distance of it being close on the wind. Needless to say, with the board all the way up we didn't fetch out of the harbor; neither did we tack very easily. But after several tacks, back winding the genoa to get around, we made it out.

A reach and run across the estuary proved very interesting with the board up. A great deal of helm was developed on the reach. Dick and Frans Maas decided that a small skeg attached in front of the rudder would help eliminate this problem. We then dropped the board, in stages, and hardened onto the wind. There was a feeling of speed not only off the wind, but also when hard on it.

On the spinnaker run back to Breskens we converged with *Tina,* who was returning to Breskens after winning the West Mersey to Ostend race. We shanghaied Willie Stettinius off her for the sail to Cowes and the Cowes-Dinard Race.

Monday and Tuesday, work continued at a feverish pace, as the interior was finished and the various pieces of equipment were hooked up. A larger gear for lifting the keel was found in northern Holland. Its delivery was expedited and its installation completed by 2:00 A.M. Wednesday. It had to work now, for our time at the yard had run out. Our departure from Breskens was at 3:00 A.M. Wednesday, in time to catch the favorable tide.

The trip was windless and uneventful until we entered the Solent, where we ran out of fuel. This wasn't totally unexpected, for our rough fuel consumption calculations had indicated that it would be close. We sailed into Cowes just in time for a spree of necessary shopping before the stores closed Thursday.

The start of the Cowes-Dinard Race Friday noon was in a flat calm. Luckily we had had a mechanic "bleed" the fuel line and engine of air that morning. This is one of the inherent problems in running out of fuel with a diesel engine; one cannot simply fill the tank to start up again. Even so, our engine problems were not over. The shifting mechanism was stuck in reverse! As there was no wind and the tide was so strong that everyone was in danger of being carried over the line before the start, we not only powered out of Cowes backward, but continued to mill around the starting area in reverse.

As the two divisions of Class III got away it became obvious that we would have to anchor, for the rules require engines to be off prior to one's preparatory gun 5 minutes before the start. The rest of our class was jockeying into position to do the same thing. We anchored in a good position a short distance from the line. It being, theoretically, a running start, we turned *Red Rooster* around and anchored by the stern, with our bow headed for the line and with spinnaker gear all set forward. The idea was to set the spinnaker prior to the gun, getting it to draw, and then to break the anchor loose just before the gun. In this way we would cross the line just after the gun. (We didn't want to play it too close, for being over the line early would be disastrous. The light wind and strong tide would make it nearly impossible to recross the line. This did happen to two boats, and they lost hours trying to restart correctly.)

Unfortunately, our scheme developed one flaw; otherwise we certainly would have had a perfect start. As we settled into our anchored position, and just before our 5-minute gun, four of our competitors chose to anchor in a line directly in front of us. They all anchored by the bow. When the starting gun was fired those four boats were pulling up their anchors. They then had to turn around and head for the line. We were in the frustrating position of having to wait for them to clear out of our way, for, already heading in the right direction, we would have been on top of them in no time once we had broken our anchor out. This would have been pure folly; with the limited maneuverability we could never have gotten through safely.

As it was we didn't fare too badly, for we had the spinnaker set as the anchor was hauled aboard—no small task in itself. To break it out we had to haul *Red Rooster* backward against the strong current. This not only was a physically difficult job, requiring more speed than the genoa winch could give, but also caused Dick considerable trouble in keeping *Red Rooster* headed in the desired direction.

As we got clear of the line our attention turned to bringing the swing keel up and closing the slot. The larger gear enabled us to lift the keel, but not without considerable effort. One person could take about 25 turns (depending on the person's condition) on the handle before tiring. It was going to be important to be able to raise and lower the swing keel in a hurry, especially when we were racing around the buoys. We developed a chain gang effect, with one or two people cranking at a time. After 25 turns a new cranker or crankers would take over. The result was a stream of people rushing below, either through the forward hatch or down the companionway, and another continuous line of people staggering on deck to relieve someone for his turn below.

With the keel up and the curtain closed we definitely moved ahead of our class and began to pass those who had started ahead of us.

The southwest wind filled in as we passed the forts off Portsmouth, allowing for a fast reach out to the Nab Tower. *Red Rooster* was going to be fast reaching, for we walked over boats ahead of us and widened the distance on our class behind. Upon rounding the Nab, with only a few boats ahead, we hardened onto the wind and

Red Rooster *at start of Cowes–Dinard Race. Note rudder in partially raised position, high aspect ratio main, and "Tall Boy" spinnaker staysail.*

set across the Channel. To our delight and, as we learned later, a great many people's amazement, we not only outfooted our class, but outpointed them as well.

During the evening, with the wind lightening, we found ourselves amongst the leaders, all Class I boats. *Coriolan, Crusade, Ragamuffin,* and *Phantom* were all nearby. The only Class II boat around was *Mercedes III.* She was hull down to leeward. As darkness descended the wind swung into the south, putting us in an even better position.

Throughout the night we had a close battle with Geof Pattinson's *Phantom.* As the wind shifted back and forth we sometimes closed on her, and other times she pulled out on us; never could she pull away. It was a very encouraging night for us, but undoubtedly a discouraging one on board *Phantom.* Not only was she one of the British Admiral's Cup boats, but she was a bigger boat, in Class I, and yet couldn't leave us astern.

During the morning we rounded the Casquets and hoped the wind would return to the southwest and fill in to enable us to get past Les Hanois before the tide turned against us there. At its height it flowed at 6 knots, something we would much rather leave for those behind us. The race is often won or lost here. The shortest course is close to the Casquets and Les Hanois, but should one miss the favorable current, the longer offshore route, where there is less current, is often more desirable. The offshore route is the conventional one; it is safer in that it gives a wide berth to the rocks that make up Les Hanois, a dangerous place on a dark stormy night.

The wind held in the south and the tide turned against us before we rounded Les Hanois. We could see *Crusade, Coriolan,* and *Ragamuffin* standing offshore ahead of us. With *Phantom* just to weather, we tacked in toward Guernsey, hoping to avoid the foul tide by staying in close to shore. We led *Phantom* in amongst the rocks and islands off the northwest shore of Guernsey. It was one of those rare bright days, and with the water so clear we had no trouble navigating by the color of the water. We did have to make a few detours from our beating courses due to obstacles in our path, but it was well worth it, for we stayed out of the worst of the head current. This was obvious as we observed the flow of water past lobster buoys on our offshore tacks compared to those closer to the shore. Once, when we headed in behind one of the small islands, a local fisherman waved frantically to us not to go in. After another look at the chart and a visual survey of the water ahead we continued on through. Later we heard from one of the boats that had stopped at St. Peter Port on the other end of Guernsey on the way back to England that there was talk around town of a red boat that had sailed in places the local fishermen only go at the highest tide and with no wind.

As we worked out toward Les Hanois we discovered that we were in a counter-current. *Phantom* discovered this earlier than we did and took full advantage of it, fetching past the rocks with ample room to spare. We were slower to appreciate that we had a counter-current and stayed closer to shore than necessary. Thus we had to really pinch to windward in order to sneak around the outermost rocks forming Les Hanois. It was nip and tuck as to whether or not we would make it. We were now in the head tide, and to tack offshore would put the current pushing us sideways. With Frank van Beuningen working us to windward, Dick watching the approaching rocks, and the rest of us poised for a quick tack, we did sneak past.

Ragamuffin, about a mile off the point, was horrified to see *Phantom* and ourselves come up on her so fast. She was fighting the strongest part of the current.

The final leg in to the finish off Dinard was a spinnaker reach. We were afraid all along that it would be a race against time. With evening and the change of tide the wind was sure to drop. Could we finish before the tide turned against us again, leaving us becalmed and fighting a strong head current?

Our fears were justified: when the tide turned with us the wind slowly decreased. The difficulty of the current is that as one approaches the land its direction swings from pushing you forward from just off your stern to pushing you from nearly abeam. Thus, with very little wind, we were pointing toward the finish, but our actual movement over the bottom was nearly sideways. To allow for this we held high of our course. We could see *Crusade, Coriolan, Ragamuffin,* and *Noryema VII* approaching the line just before dark. It was going to be close as to which boat would finish first, and difficult to keep from being swept past the line without going over it. *Noryema* saw *Crusade* and *Coriolan* drop their spinnakers ahead and harden nearly onto the wind in an attempt to prevent themselves from being swept on the wrong side of the line. So *Noryema* held higher earlier, trying to judge the progress of current moving her sideways versus her forward movement.

Crusade finally crossed first, followed slowly by the other four. *Pacha* and *Phantom,* just ahead of us, were having a close battle to keep from being swept on the wrong side of the line. We kept holding higher and higher, with much discussion as to how high to hold. The problem was made more difficult by the changing strength of the wind—not that it ever got very strong, but at times our forward speed actually picked up.

As we approached the finish line *Pacha* and *Phantom* were desperately trying to inch across the finish line. Both boats were being swept sideways fast. They both needed a little forward motion to enable them to be swept across the line; otherwise they would be swept past on the wrong side of the buoy. Just at the critical moment *Pacha,* getting a breath of air, moved up on *Phantom,* blanketing her completely. *Pacha*'s way carried her across the line sideways, while *Phantom* was swept past on the wrong side of the buoy. Down went her anchor and stayed there, while she watched a number of boats finish ahead of her.

We had our own nerve-wracking time in threading the finish line, but did so successfully, being sixth boat across.

The strong current and light wind played havoc with others as well. *Prospect of Whitby,* Arthur Slater's brand new Sparkman and Stephens design, was carried on the wrong side of one of the Minquiers buoys. She was forced to anchor for several hours, unable to get back to the buoy.

Unfortunately for us the wind filled in from astern and brought the fleet in right behind us. But they too had problems. With the wind came a very thick fog, closing off visibility altogether. Many a boat spent considerable time finding the finish line. Once across, the problem of groping into harbor was overpowering. Most boats anchored. *Mercedes III* ended up motoring in tight circles around a buoy for three hours before attempting, with semi-visibility, the passage in.

We felt pleased with our performance: sixth overall, first in Class II. Certainly we were noticed by the other Admiral's Cup teams; all of England's and Australia's Admiral's Cup boats participated.

We took a leisurely trip back to England, stopping one night at Sark. A real centerboarder is a great cruising boat. We moved right in to the beach, tying up to some rocks—which enabled us to get ashore without bothering to pump up the dinghy. After the Fastnet Race I joined Dick and his family for ten days of cruising the southern coast of Brittany including the Gulf of Morbihan. It was just the boat for "gunkholing" around; with the keel up we drew less than 3 feet! Many times local yachtsmen were flabbergasted when, advising us that there wouldn't be enough water for us to lie at our chosen anchorage at low water, they learned that we drew less than their much smaller boats. We not only tied up to shore numerous times, but went up rivers and into harbors much too shallow for even a conventional centerboarder. When nosing around shallow places we normally left a foot of the keel down. This assisted our maneuverability. It was also a method of avoiding being stuck aground should we hit bottom. We would merely raise the keel and back off. But during our cruising we never did touch bottom.

Back in England we went up to the Berthon Yard in Lymington. There were some major problems that had to be rectified before the Channel Race—in 8 days' time. Allen Boyde was on the spot, quickly understanding the problems, offering sound suggestions and the help needed. This was reassuring, for, though the English yards build wooden boats of extremely fine workmanship, they seem, from my limited experience, not to have the competence to meet the problems of today with today's technology.

We were lifted out on a travel crane, where we lowered the swing keel all the way. We calibrated the gear, indicating how much the board was down. Previously, we could only tell by looking through the plexiglass centerboard trunk top. Twenty-five turns on the crank moved the keel about one foot. It required 175 swings to raise or lower the keel the full distance. There seemed still to be problems with the gear mechanism, for it was still very difficult to work.

The rudder was removed and cut down, and the forward end of the centerboard box had to be fixed, for some 6 inches of fiberglass had been smashed. This had apparently happened in Breskens when the cable slipped off the drum and the keel swung a few feet forward on the centerboard pin. We were launched again Friday night, in time to enter the two day races Saturday and Sunday.

Saturday morning the wind was very light from the east. All of the British and Australian Admiral's Cup boats were out. This could be a very interesting race—and so it was! The first leg was a run with the tide to the west. We messed up the spinnaker at the start, but finally got it going and, with the keel up and the slot closed, began to move up with the leaders. About halfway to the mark the wind came in from the southwest, making it a beat the rest of the way. We had several busy minutes changing the spinnaker to the #1 genoa and lowering the keel at the same time. It was imperative that the curtain be completely withdrawn whenever the keel was moved. Should the curtain not be withdrawn, the raising or lowering of the keel would force the curtain out of its guiding grooves along the inside edge of the centerboard box, thus making it inoperative. The keel would also become stationary, unable to move up or down.

We rounded the first mark about fifth and ran back to the east. With the tide still flooding to the west, the fleet edged in toward the mainland shore, trying to stay out of the strongest current. *Noryema VII* was just ahead of us. Suddenly she stopped dead in the water. She was well offshore, but the bar that extends off that point is quite long and very shallow. *Noryema*'s crew was able to head her toward deep water, but was unable to heel the boat enough to get her into it. Within a matter of minutes most of the crew was overboard, standing in water up to their waists, trying to push her off. The

Ragamuffin *with Graham Newland at the helm*

Ragamuffin *(left) and* Red Rooster, *having just rounded a windward mark. Crew by* Red Rooster's *mast are poised to drop through the forehatch for their turn at cranking the swing keel up.*

falling tide left them hard aground. Later on, people waded out from shore or even rode out on their bicycles to take a look at the big ocean racer. Hours later the tide refloated her, and she returned to Cowes with harm done only to her crew's pride.

As the rest of us crossed a line between Cowes and Southampton, the original wind returned. It seemed that the southwest wind was in the western part of the Solent, but was having a very hard and slow time pushing the easterly out of the eastern end. As we crossed from one breeze to the other the wind was very light and spotty. The middle boat of three, all within 30 yards of each other, was just as likely to get her own breeze and sail away from the other two. The wind held in the east, making two close fetches and a run to the finish.

As we rounded the last buoy off Rye, *Ragamuffin* was leading, with *Phantom* right on her heels. We were third with *Prospect of Whitby* right behind us. On board *Red Rooster* there was a great deal of commotion, with some people hurrying below decks and others staggering on deck to help trim the sails as the spinnaker was set, the keel raised, and the slot closed.

By now the tide had turned to the east. *Ragamuffin* and *Phantom* were having a real fight, *Phantom* trying to work up on *Ragamuffin*'s quarter to bother her wind. *Ragamuffin* kept edging higher with *Phantom* to keep her from doing what she wanted. This jockeying around brought the two boats in close to shore off Castle Point. This wasn't too bad, because it got them out of the building head tide out in deeper water, but they would have to be careful to stay off the ledge that inhabits the water off this point.

We had pulled away from *Prospect of Whitby* during the run, and our attention was fixed on the two boats ahead. Suddenly *Ragamuffin* stopped. She had found the ledge. *Phantom* did a quick gybe and headed for deep water, waving and offering advice to *Ragamuffin*. She got some 20 yards outside of *Ragamuffin* before stopping on the other end of the same ledge.

We watched with glee as first *Ragamuffin* and then *Phantom* ran aground. A short discussion erupted on board as to whether to go inside or outside the grounded boats. With them drawing over 7 feet, our 2 feet 9 inches would be no problem if we held our course and sailed by between the two grounded boats and shore. I could just picture Graham Newland's face as we sailed by!

We held our course with the light wind dead astern. Much of our attention was on *Phantom*'s and *Ragamuffin*'s efforts to get off. There were spinnaker poles over the side and two or three people hanging from booms. Neither boat was very sociable as we slid by. Just as we got past the two grounded boats we ran into trouble ourselves. The wind changed 180 degrees and was now coming from dead ahead!

Not only did we have to get the spinnaker down and the genoa up and trimmed, but also we had to retract the curtain and drop the keel. Besides all this we had to tack, for we were headed for shore. Working at frantic speed we got everything accomplished, and the keel was almost all the way down as we pulled abeam of *Ragamuffin*, still hard aground, heading for deeper water. That was our downfall: we were too fast. We had gotten the keel too far down, and it came to rest right opposite *Ragamuffin*'s on the same rock.

As we hit, the cranking changed directions and we were off in a very short time. But we had lost all forward motion, and with the tide at right angles to our heading and the very light wind we were carried down onto first *Ragamuffin* and then *Phantom*. As we approached each boat broadside their activity changed from trying to get off to protecting their port sides.

During all this, *Prospect of Whitby* kept well clear offshore. She picked up the southwest breeze which filled in out there first and romped up to the finish line, finishing first by a good margin.

We quickly consulted the rule book concerning hitting a grounded vessel. Since we didn't really believe that our contact with *Ragamuffin* and *Phantom* was a result of our coming to their rescue, we withdrew from the race.

Later that evening I learned that when we ran aground it was the first time during the race that the crews on board *Ragamuffin* and *Phantom* smiled. This simple statement, having no relation to the upcoming Admiral's Cup races, was in fact an excellent indication of the seriousness of the coming series.

The Australian team, being the defender, was determined to return the Cup to Sydney. The British were equally determined to bring it back to England. The rivalry and competition between the two teams was sure to lift the overall level of competition to an extremely high point. We hoped we could match this level with *Red Rooster*, although we had very little hope of the American team doing well as a team. Our teammates were Dick Nye's new *Carina*, designed to the C.C.A. rule by McCurdy, and Tom Watson's *Palawan*, of Sparkman and Stephens design in 1964. The father-son Nye combination is well acquainted with Admiral's Cup competition, having competed in the series before with a previous *Carina*. They made a considerable effort to improve the C.C.A.-designed *Carina*'s R.O.R.C. rating. Of major significance was the shortening of the foot of her mainsail. *Palawan* apparently had no changes made, nor was there any attempt to improve her R.O.R.C. rating. Her rating was exceedingly high in relation to R.O.R.C. boats of equal size.

Carina, we felt, would be able to hold her own. *Palawan,* we felt, would never be able to sail up to her rating. We were optimistic about *Red Rooster*'s ability to be a leader; our goal was to be the Admiral's Cup boat with the highest number of individual points.

France came in with a strong, organized team. Italy brought a well-sailed team of hot boats to England. Germany and Holland were geared up once again with full teams, as were Finland and Argentina. Spain and Bermuda fielded teams of two boats each.

Most of the competing teams and boats were not geared up to the level of the British and Australian teams. This wasn't going to detract from the series. Thirty-one boats were to compete, the largest Admiral's Cup fleet yet. Each boat was crewed by people eager to sail their best, hoping against hope that *they* would win. The prestige alone of being part of this series is exciting, for the Admiral's Cup competition receives the brightest spotlight during Cowes Week. If it continues along the course it has been following, it will be indisputably the best competition for ocean racing anywhere in the world.

Carina *on the Solent with R.O.R.C. main*

The need is there, and the competitors want it and in fact are far ahead of the organization running it. If the organization can catch up and run the series in a first-class professional manner, then nothing will equal the Admiral's Cup.

The conditions for the start of the Sunday race were the same as the day before, running before a light easterly with the tide. We made a good start offshore, but today those boats in on the Island shore got a better slant of wind. *Quiver V* and *Phantom* led us around the mark. *Prospect of Whitby* was right on our heels. The play again was to stay as close to shore as one dared while beating back to the east. It was pleasing to work to windward of them on the first leg in toward shore. The four of us made several tacks away from and then back toward shore without changing positions. During one bad tack *Prospect* got past us. Racing like this just doesn't leave room for mistakes.

The Beaulieu River (pronounced Buley by the English) empties into the Solent right along where we were beating. The river's channel follows the shore line for perhaps three-quarters of a mile, with a very shallow sand bar forming its offshore shoulder or bank. Most of the time this bar is well under water, but there are places that are exposed at low water. The water was about three-quarters high as we approached the Beaulieu River entrance.

Much debate was held between our navigator, two local lads sailing with us, and Dick as to whether we could cross the bar and get into the river's channel or not, and how much keel we could afford to lose. At some point we would lose more distance sliding sideways than we could make up by getting out of the head tide.

We held on, getting the keel up to a draft of 5 feet. It was interesting to see boats following behind us flop over and head offshore while we kept on in, seemingly undisturbed by the sand bar. *Rainbow*, the beautifully sailed New Zealand boat that had just won the 1969 One Ton Cup, decided that they could go anywhere we could. They hadn't heard that we had a swing keel. They were sure that we must draw at least 7 feet, while they draw only a little over 6 feet. Before long they tacked; their depth sounder was bouncing around on 7 feet.

We made it over the sand bar, having no idea how close we came to hitting bottom. A few short tacks in the river's channel brought us back into the Solent ahead of *Quiver* and *Prospect*.

The wind changed back and forth and boats changed positions now and again. Somewhere along the line *Prospect* ran into trouble and retired from the race. It was a twice-around course. As we started up along the shore off Beaulieu River again—the sand bar was well exposed this time—I noticed a boat high and dry well up on the beach. This seemed strange, for I hadn't seen any boats on the beach during the earlier trip along this stretch. After a closer inspection of the boat with binoculars I discovered it was *Mercedes III*. Much to their chagrin, they spent some 13 hours waiting for the tide to get them afloat again.

That evening we returned to Berthon's for two days of relaxing and preparing for the real thing.

Thursday the crew gathered. In addition to Dick and me there was Jim Anderson, a naval architect by training who had recently joined Dick's design organization; John Carter; Jim Mullans; and Skip Allen, the younger of the Allen brothers from Southern California, each of whom has skippered a boat to Transpac wins and each of whom holds a Congressional Cup trophy. Skip was just in from Denmark, where he had been sailing in the first Soling world championship.

That afternoon we went out for a sail to acquaint the recent ar rivals with *Red Rooster*'s equipment. *Palawan* was out practicing as well. *Carina* was scheduled to join us but, as we learned later, was marooned on dry land in Portsmouth. The travel crane that had lifted her out was broken and she could not get into the water.

Since racing the previous weekend Dick had been toying with the notion that we could use some good extra hands, especially during the day races. We found that there was more than enough to keep six people overly busy when racing around the buoys. Skip knew of two of his Soling cohorts who were in Cowes looking for a berth. We returned to shore and went looking for them.

Friday morning Warwick (Commodore) Tompkins and Taylor

Grant, both from California, joined our crew. The start of the Channel Race, off Portsmouth, was at 6:30 Friday evening. The wind was light, out of the northeast, making it questionable whether we could fetch out past the forts without tacking. To add to the turmoil of boats milling around the starting area, the tide was flowing out very fast. As each class neared its preparatory gun, 5 minutes before its start, most of the boats powered well away from the line. Then, with the preparatory gun, their engines were turned off and they headed for the line, being carried toward it mainly by the tide. The Admiral's Cup boats started as a group first. We were nearly on the line as our starting gun went, very close to the offshore end of the line. We were in a safe position with clear wind, but at the wrong end of the line. The current was much stronger in toward shore.

The course from the forts to the Owers Light Vessel was a definite beat. We stood on out toward the English Channel. Others tacked in toward shore, and looked good. As darkness approached, *Kialoa,* a 73-foot yawl from Los Angeles, roared by to leeward, and *American Eagle,* the 12-meter-turned-ocean-racer, sliced past us to windward.

The visibility turned from haze to thick fog. During the night it got thicker. The night was made even more eerie by rain and electrical storms. The wind came and went in circles, finally filling in from the south.

The Channel Race course had been altered slightly. The Royal Sovereign Light Vessel, off Beachy Head, had been replaced by Basurelle Light Vessel, further to the southeast; next came the Le Havre Light Vessel.

We approached Basurelle Light Vessel under spinnaker in a light westerly. We could see *Kialoa* and 12 others—Class I boats, we hoped —heading for Le Havre. By mid-morning we too were reaching for Le Havre. Some boats held high of the rhumb line; we headed directly for the next mark. As we closed with the French coast the tide turned in our favor, lifting the apparent wind speed considerably and bringing it in from the southwest, as well as building up a considerable chop.

As we sneaked past the high awesome cliffs surrounding the cape

Channel Race

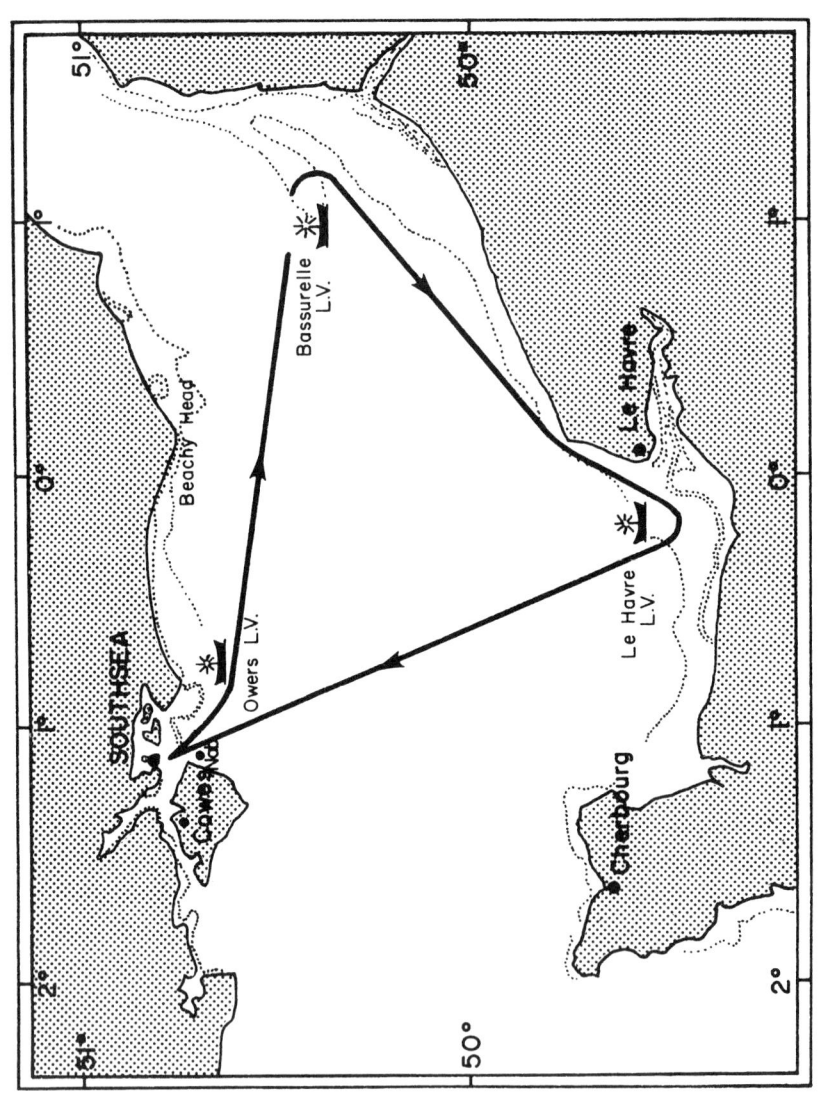

we were down to #3 genoa and 6 rolls in the main. The Le Havre Light was dead to windward. Those boats that had held high on their courses earlier would be in a good position now. I heard later that very few actually fetched Le Havre. Most had the same beat we did. Others, who fell below the rhumb line trying to carry spinnakers, had a very long beat.

As the tide slackened, the apparent wind slackened, and we increased sail. We rounded the Le Havre Light Ship—which is a buoy during the summer months—two hours after the tide changed. The reach back to Portsmouth was fast and uneventful. At dawn we saw a boat, some 2 miles on our weather quarter. We had no idea who she was or where she came from. Our only concern was to leave her behind. But it wasn't that easy. And no wonder, for, as we closed on the English coast, we recognized her to be *Quiver V*, a new Class I Nicholson design with Peter Nicholson on board. Our presence was being felt; rumor had it that we had surfed across the Channel. We led them around the Nab Tower and had them still on our quarter as we crossed the finish line Sunday morning.

We were the 16th boat to finish. *Rainbow* won on corrected time. *Ragamuffin* came in second, beating us by one minute. *Prospect of Whitby*, *Mercedes III*, *Phantom*, and *Noryema VII* followed.

As for the Admiral's Cup standings after the first race, the defenders had a substantial lead. Their boats had finished first, fourth, and seventh, accumulating 168 points. The Italian team, surprising a good many people, totalled 130 points. And the U.S. and British teams tied for third with 120 points each, placing 2, 8, and 26 for the U.S. and 3, 5, and 28 for Britain.

The fleet slowly returned to Cowes to recuperate for the forthcoming week. Even though there are races each day, only two of them affect the Admiral's Cup: the Britannia Cup Tuesday and the New York Yacht Club Challenge Cup Thursday. These were the only day races we were going to enter. The other days would be spent resting and preparing.

The Britannia Cup's start was to the west in a light northerly. Half the fleet stayed on the Island shore or mid-Channel, while the other half hugged the mainland shore. We stuck it out down the middle. Nearly everyone anchored for a spell before the wind filled in from the north, reaching those on the mainland side of the Solent first. We finally reached the windward mark, having crossed to the Island shore and played touch and go along the beach. As the second time around began, the wind filled in strongly from the southwest and continued to build for the remainder of the race.

Prospect of Whitby won on corrected time, the Italian *Mabelle* came in second, and we finished third. Although the Australians could only muster 6, 7, and 13, they increased their lead over the Italians, and only the British team, with a 1, 8, 10, gained on them. The U.S. took over sole possession of fourth place with a 4, 14, 20. The British moved into second and the Italians dropped to third place.

It is not often that a complete day of Cowes Week passes without one race. Often gales have kept the smaller classes or the more timid on their moorings. But on Wednesday, the Squadron signalled postponement after postponement, and finally called the whole thing off, for there was truly *no* wind.

Thursday made up for it by being a perfect sailing day. The racing started in a rock-steady easterly of about 15 m.p.h. Our course took us east of Cowes first, to the Warners Buoy, a mile east of the forts, and then a long leg to the Lymington Spit well to the west of Cowes and back to the finish line, a distance of 35 miles.

The American team was a far cry from the organization of the British, Australian, French, and Italian teams, all with their sailing uniforms. Before the race, Taylor had decided that we on *Red Rooster*'s crew should have our own uniform. Just before the start all seven of us disappeared below decks to get into our uniforms, leaving Dick to sail the boat by himself. On cue we emerged through the fore hatch and companionway to the surprised delight of Dick and the astonishment of those sailing nearby. Each of us had a hat like Dick's and white T shirts. On the front, marked in red, was "Red Rooster." On the back was "Carter's Factory Team."

With the tide going to the west at the start, the inshore end of the line was definitely favored. There was considerable jockeying around

Red Rooster *running over sandbank with swing keel raised. Note depth sounder (boat hook) off leeward rail.*

as we tried to find an opening as close to the inshore end as possible —which is literally 20 yards from the beach. After a couple of tight squeezes we got away to a good start. For the beat out to the Warners, we were sailing with *Koomooloo, Prospect of Whitby, Mabelle,* and *Phantom* the whole way. At one point we made a bad tack, slowing us just enough for *Koomooloo* to get by. It took another boat, racing for the N.Y.Y.C. Cup but not an Admiral's Cup boat, to cover *Koomooloo* before we could get ahead of her. The Admiral's Cup racing doesn't allow for even one mistake. And with competition as keen as it is, it is a shame to have the Admiral's Cup races held as part of other races. These, with time, enough complaints from competitors, and organizational awareness, will eventually be separated.

The run to Lymington Spit saw nearly a quarter of the fleet split away from the rhumb line and reach up, standing well in to the Portsmouth coast. Among the leaders of this group were *Phantom, Runn,* and *Prospect of Whitby.* They looked very good as they reached in, and it was tempting to follow suit. We held to our rhumb line course down the middle of the Solent and began to open out on *Koomooloo,* who was following us. She decided to split the difference, going in to shore only half way. For a while she looked as though she were pulling ahead. But in the long run none of the boats that held high got enough tide or sailed fast enough to make up the difference in their longer course. We gained on them considerably as the courses converged again off Southampton for the continuation of the run off the mainland shore. *Noryema VII* led us along the shallow mainland coast, while offshore the keel boats had to buck a stronger tide. Our inshore route paid great dividends.

We did have a few anxious moments when, some hundred yards offshore of us, *Rubin* came to a slow but permanent stop. The whole fleet immediately veered to the left, giving the shore a wider berth. We held our course, and held our breaths as we passed well inside of *Rubin,* just in case we touched as well.

Taylor Grant developed his own method of shallow water sounding. Lying on the foredeck he swung the boat hook, some 12 feet long, forward and down. Several times he hit bottom at 3/4 boat hook length; most of the time he couldn't reach bottom. We never hit, and gained appreciably on those out in deeper water as the tide was picking up considerable strength.

The beat back to the finish line saw us overtake a couple more boats. We crossed 19th. After all the calculations were completed, we had won. *Mabelle* came in second, 17 seconds behind us. Then came the formidable *Ragamuffin* and *Koomooloo,* with *Prospect* and *Phantom* fifth and sixth.

It was good racing, with many finely sailed boats from a variety of countries. During the day races no one country dominated the top positions. The first 7 boats in the Britannia Cup represented 6 different nations. For the New York Yacht Club Challenge Cup the first 7 boats represented 5 countries, not a bad spread for such racing. The trick to winning as a team is to place consistently high with all three boats. The Australians were doing this once again, as the following chart indicates. The British were the only other team that had any consistency in placing high.

	Australia	*Britain*	*Italy*	*U.S.A.*	*Germany*
Channel Race	1, 4, 7	3, 5, 28	6, 9, 16	2, 8, 26	11, 14, 18
Britannia Cup	6, 7, 13	1, 8, 10	2, 4, –	3, 14, 18	11, 15, –
N.Y.Y.C.	3, 4, 10	5, 6, 9	2, 13, 19	1, 8, 24	7, 12, 15
TOTALS SO FAR	317	273	250	244	206

Going into the Fastnet Race the U.S. team stood fourth, 73 points behind the leading Australian team. The Australians didn't have the Cup in their hands yet, for the all-important Fastnet Race counts treble points. *Red Rooster* held a slight lead in the individual total with 120 points, followed by *Ragamuffin* and *Prospect of Whitby* with 116 points each and *Mabelle* with 112 points. Again, the top 4 boats represented 4 countries.

Friday was a busy day in Cowes for us, obtaining food and fixing gear, and at noon *Red Rooster* was hauled to have her bottom scrubbed. As we were going back into the water, while hanging in the travel lift over the opening of water that we were to be launched in, the keel started moving down all by itself. Fortunately we had lowered it most of the way to clean it; now it hung all the way down and the gears to lift it spun freely. We gingerly moved *Red Rooster* back over solid land and then lowered the hull, at the same time moving it forward to enable the keel to swing back up into the centerboard box. The problem of fixing it was paramount. We did not know which of the gears had broken, nor why, nor whether it could be fixed. Time was of the essence, for the Fastnet start was the next morning at 10:15.

Had this happened two years previously there wouldn't have been a prayer of fixing it. But in the last two years Cowes has taken a giant step forward in ability to cope with big boats, their gear, and problems in anything other than wood. The yard was extremely cooperative and helpful even though it already had a tight schedule in hauling and launching boats and last-minute problems before the Fastnet.

Once safely on dry land we removed the gear covers. This revealed a badly marred and twisted pin that had supported the two reduction gears that turned the main drum. The pin had been supported only in the middle, between the two gears, with no support at either of the pin's ends. The loads and strains on the whole mechanism were too much for this precariously balanced pin. They must have been tremendous, for the pin was 2 inches in diameter and made of stainless steel.

The only way to work on this was to remove the whole gear box, something we were very hesitant to do, for it had caused considerable problems when initially installed back in Breskens. But there was no other way, so Jim and I went about removing the box, even though we weren't sure it could be fixed in time or that we could put it back together.

Our prolonged stay on land caused considerable comment and speculation from those who came by. We were vague in our replies, indicating no troubles with our keel. One way or another we would be at the line for the start, even if we had to sail the race without being able to raise the keel. It would do no harm to leave it down, just slow us down off the wind, but we certainly didn't want to give our competitors a psychological advantage in knowing that we couldn't raise our keel.

The yard's mechanical shop turned out to study the problem with Jim and Dick around 4:30. Once they realized that overtime wouldn't be a problem they settled down to some solutions. With the problem well understood they departed for supper. Upon returning they had planned a course of action—one that should not only work, but work in time. That was assuming Jim and I could get the gear box connected back up to the keel and boat.

There was nothing we could do, so after a hearty supper ashore we turned in, leaving instructions to awaken us when they finished or when problems arose. Around 4:30 Saturday morning a thunderstorm awoke Jim and me. We were a bit concerned, for the estimate of when the gears would be ready for us had been between two and three. We went to investigate and found those still there tired, but with big smiles, for they had nearly finished.

Jim and I took over the task at 5:00 A.M., and amazingly enough it went together without much trouble. Within 2 hours we had the keel securely hoisted and were happily eating breakfast.

The Admiral's Cup boats started together and last. We had the whole fleet to catch. The wind was light from the east, providing a spinnaker run down the Solent. Light fickle winds and foul tides plagued the fleet as we all inched westward. Everyone's concern was to get past Portland Bill Saturday night before the tide turned eastward. Those that made it fell flat at Start Point where, Sunday morning, over a hundred boats gathered for a new start. During the early morning hours our headway seemed to stop, and with a head tide over went the anchor. Much to everyone's amazement *Red Rooster* swung around lying on the anchor heading to the east. Our headway had apparently ceased only because the counter-current was carrying us to the west. We seemed to be in the lead of this group, up with big Class I boats. But there, not far behind, was *Rainbow,* a Class III boat. In the fickle southerly we pulled away from the mass of boats behind with our own breeze. *Coriolan* and *Crusade* fell down on top of us; *Crusade,* trying to carry her spinnaker, was headed in for Plymouth. *Coriolan* got trimmed properly and promptly pulled ahead and to windward. As the afternoon wore on, the wind headed us some, forcing us in toward Falmouth. With us for the short tacking out to the Lizard were the big German sloops *Diana* and *Rubin; Phantom* and *Ragamuffin* were also nearby. Off Falmouth a man in a small outboard-driven dory told us that *American Eagle* had cleared the Manacles Rocks only an hour and three-quarters ahead of us. As far as he had been able to see, we were about sixth boat-for-boat. This really lifted our spirits. But what made the race, regardless of the end results, was to have *Kialoa* cross our bow a mere three-quarters of a mile away as we approached Land's End. The Californians became extremely excited. They knew most of *Kialoa*'s crew and had sailed on her themselves. There was talk that *Kialoa*'s tack, just to weather of us, was to cover us.

Palawan was ahead of us as we approached Land's End, but made an unnecessary tack and overstood the rounding enough to let us pass. Next mark was Fastnet Rock.

A close spinnaker reach proved interesting as the wind increased but then swung into the west and, by morning, into the northwest. Later, against all weather forecasts, it continued into the north.

The seas were big compared to the wind. Most boats within sight were unable to make any headway when they tacked to the southwest. The result was that most of the fleet headed north. When the wind under the Irish Coast veered to the north, those boats that had held on the port tack were able to fetch Fastnet Rock. Three such boats were *Carina,* who had had previous success under the Irish Coast, *Palawan,* and *Crusade.* We made better progress than most on the starboard tack and headed to the southwest mid-morning Monday, getting to the south of the rhumb line in anticipation of the predicted sou'wester.

An almost unbelievable phenomenon occurred Monday night when we were still some 50 miles away from the Rock. We could see its

Red Rooster's *winning crew:* (*back row*) *Bill Green, John Carter, Taylor Grant,* (*front row*) *Sandy Weld, Jim Anderson, Skip Allen, Commodore Tomkins, Dick Carter*

loom in the sky. The light itself has a visibility of 18 miles. It was a long time between our first sight of the light and our closing in on the Rock at 1320 Tuesday.

Ahead of us we could see *Phantom* and *Pacha;* a good distance behind us were *Mabelle, Prospect, Quiver, Diana,* and *Zeetort.* The full northwesterly provided us with a fast spinnaker run for Bishop's Rock. The wind was practically dead astern, but the seas were off our weather quarter. This combination kept us from catching many good rides on the waves. Most of those ahead of us held high in an attempt at tacking downwind. Had we gybed and sailed in exactly the same direction as the waves, with the wind just over our quarter, we would have had a real ride.

Even so, *Red Rooster* proved she could run. *Ragamuffin* lopped off over one hour on *Carina* on this leg between Fastnet Rock and Bishop's Rock, but she did not gain on us. During the run *Phantom,* tacking off to the south, dropped back. The only boats to catch us were *Diana* and *Rubin.*

As we approached the Bishop Wednesday morning the wind dropped considerably and came in from the north. The trip in from Bishop's Rock to the finish could only be one of constant fear of the wind's dropping altogether. The big question was what would happen once we were past the Lizard.

Diana and *Rubin* spent the day getting past us, but once the wind went really light we overtook them again. *Phantom* was determined to catch us during the day. Time after time she hardened up and then reached back to our course under her reaching spinnaker. She just couldn't gain. Off the Lizard she got into tidal problems and dropped back further. We stayed in close to shore from the Lizard on in, and to our good fortune carried an evening offshore breeze the whole way in.

The initial computations Thursday morning made it a close contest as to whether we would beat *Crusade* on corrected time or not. *Mabelle* was the last boat to finish Thursday morning. As time passed and the waters off Plymouth remained glassy, our hope of winning began to build. *Rainbow*—our biggest concern—was reportedly seen off the Lizard. By Thursday noon all areas, from the Fastnet to the Bishop in to the finish line, reported flat calms. Boats were stranded, drifting in circles, from the Lizard out to Bishop's Rock and further back. Some crews anchored, others fished, others played cards. It was an unfortunate way to have a race end.

Although the battle ended for many before they reached shore, it continued on shore for *Crusade* and *Red Rooster*. The computer finally calculated that *Red Rooster* beat *Crusade* by 68 seconds. *Crusade*'s skipper/owner and navigator disputed the time given them by the finish line officials. There was a 3-minute discrepancy against them. Finally they protested the Race Committee.

Not until the awards ceremony did we know for certain that we had won the Fastnet. *Red Rooster* also won the individual point trophy. And best of all, the American team won the Admiral's Cup, thanks to having a "big boat" team all of which finished before the gates closed.

Appendix: The New Rule

A major milestone in the development of ocean racing was the creation of the new International Ocean Racing Rule (I.O.R.) in 1969. An international measurement rule had been long needed and slow in coming. Prior to 1960 prominent ocean racers formed the Offshore Rules Coordinating Committee (O.R.C.C.). This was an informal group of interested European racers who were trying to do something about measurement problems. They discussed ways of simplifying and standardizing details within the various measurement rules then in use. The O.R.C.C. had no authority to implement any changes, and the Royal Ocean Racing Club and the Cruising Club of America (the two custodians of the most widely used measurement rules) had little interest in adopting anyone else's suggestions. Each club continued to modify its own rule with slight regard to what was happening elsewhere.

The Cruising Club of America found itself custodian of the measurement rule used in major ocean racing events throughout the U.S. The club itself sponsored only the Bermuda Race and constantly debated internally as to the degree to which it should be involved in ocean racing—not necessarily a cruising man's idea of sailing. The C.C.A. was unwilling to be the national ocean racing organization, much less to be involved internationally unless the C.C.A. measurement rule was adopted.

The Royal Ocean Racing Club measurement rule, on the other hand, was supported by an outstanding organization that sponsored racing throughout northern European waters. The R.O.R.C. measurement rule was used for most ocean racing events throughout the world, with the notable exception of the United States. The English were internationally-minded as long as they were in charge. The Europeans enjoyed the benefits of the well-organized racing circuit, but felt left out with no voice on the various racing committees, and constantly took exception to the British way of running things. The R.O.R.C. dominated European racing and wouldn't consider changing its rule for any part of the C.C.A.'s rule. All this affected most those people who crossed the Atlantic to compete on the other side, whichever direction they travelled.

The level of competition during the 1966 One Ton and the interest in this type of racing caught the imagination of the racing community as well as the Olympic selection committee. The committee was considering this type of racing as a new Olympic class. Late in 1966 the International Yacht Racing Union (I.Y.R.U.), the governing body of all racing rules, requested the O.R.C.C. (the only existing international body representing ocean racers) to explore the possibility of developing a single international rule. The I.Y.R.U. defined the O.R.C.C.'s objective: "the development of a truly international rule under which yachts from anywhere in the world could race with a single measurement certificate."

The real turning point for an international rule came in April 1967 at an O.R.C.C. meeting. Prominent ocean racers and racing organizations from throughout the world were invited to attend. C.C.A. Commodore Fred Adams and R.O.R.C. Commodore Mike Vernon attended the meeting. Both were impressed with the constructive discussion and the obvious desire for a single international rule. A spirit of cooperation and an unusual desire for progress were overwhelmingly evident. The commodores of the R.O.R.C. and C.C.A. committed themselves for the first time to combining the two rules. The I.Y.R.U. had provided the necessary impetus. At this meeting the vehicle to achieve the new rule was established—the Technical Committee.

This committee's task was to consider the two major rules, preserving as far as possible the objectives of both rules and the ease and simplicity of measuring under the R.O.R.C. rule. They were asked to submit to the O.R.C.C. a proposal for an international rule of measurement for offshore racing as soon as possible.

The Technical Committee was comprised of two representatives each from the C.C.A. and R.O.R.C., and one each from Scandinavian and European countries. Fred Adams selected the fabled U.S. designer Olin Stephens, who probably has designed more boats under both rules than anyone else, and Dick Carter, a tireless proponent of an international rule. Mike Vernon designated Brigadier L.R.E. Falye, who solves all the tough measurement problems for the R.O.R.C., and F.A. Haworth, one of England's top measurers. G.A. Plym represented the Scandinavian countries, and E.G. van de Stadt, the well-known designer and skipper, represented the rest of Europe. Under the chairmanship of Olin Stephens they set out to research the problems involved in bringing about one international rule. For two years the Technical Committee devoted a great deal of time and energy to analyzing all aspects of the rules, and finally produced an acceptable international rating system. This rule was adopted by the R.O.R.C. in 1969 to be used for the offshore races during the 1970 season. The C.C.A. adopted it for the 1970 Bermuda Race.

One aspect of the rule that caused considerable concern was the rating of centerboard boats. American boats have traditionally been shallow draft or centerboard. This has been a result not of the rating rule, but of the races, most of them being predominantly runs or reaches (a major flaw in U.S. racing, in my opinion). Before the adoption of the rule, several prominent U.S. designers had backed the I.O.R. even though centerboard boats fared relatively poorly under the new rule. Late in 1969 the Technical Committee met to consider the swing keel problem—*Red Rooster*'s success had caused much concern. During that meeting they stiffened the penalty placed not only on swing keel boats, but also on the conventional centerboard boats. I hope this change will be unique in the annals of the I.O.R.—in being the only time the rule was changed by overreaction and without sufficient evidence. It is debatable how much of *Red Rooster*'s 1969 success can be attributed to her ability to raise the keel completely into the hull. Still more debatable is the further penalizing of the conventional keel/centerboard boats. S.O.R.C. member clubs had quite a battle during 1970 as to whether they would use the I.O.R. in 1971 or not. Fortunately the new rule's proponents prevailed.

No rule can be perfect. And this rule has many good points, ones that will affect bilge boys as well as skippers and owners. One significant point is that the rule permits a hull to be measured out of the water, and then, once it is in the water, by merely measuring the freeboards one can determine the water line length and depth. This will greatly decrease the problems involved in measuring, cutting down the costs and time involved.

The new rule also allows for standard hull measurement. Where a stock hull can be measured, and under certain controls, all hulls will receive the same measurements. Then the only difference in the class will be the sail area used and how deep the boat is sunk in the water. This will improve class racing by eliminating the slight differences arising out of measuring similar hulls.

The I.O.R. is changing the racing scene in the U.S. more than anywhere else in the world. The best thing to come out of it has been the creation of a national offshore organization, which can only improve the calibre of U.S. racing, both long distance and day racing. Some day soon the U.S. may even have trials for such events as the Admiral's Cup and One Ton Cup competitions.

The C.C.A. and R.O.R.C. have each provided a wide variety of sound, seagoing boats for many years. It is reasonable to assume that the I.O.R. can do exactly the same, given half a chance, as well as improve the fun, excitement, and competition throughout the world.

797.124   Weld
  W   The leading
          edge

SEP 7 7